for Ann,

from your friend,

Ivonne Carson.

11/29/2018

Silence and Secrets

A Jewish Woman's Tale of Escape, Survival and Love In World War II

Yvonne Carson-Cardozo

Praise for *Silence and Secrets*

"Traveling the world to escape and survive, living a life of fear and courage, now in her 80's, Yvonne Carson-Cardozo, for the first time, reveals her hidden heart-wrenching memories. My heart was broken open as I read Silence and Secrets, an inspirational memoir of a brave woman who persevered through horrific times."

Mari J. Frank, Esq. author of *From Victim to Victor*

"The pitch-dark trail, so narrow, is almost invisible on the crest of the mountain. Young Yvonne is injured, hungry, and so exhausted that she walks in a stupor, well aware that one wrong step means death from the fall. And going back means death from the Nazis. What saves her is an indomitable will to overcome and to survive, and the courage of some truly humane individuals whose sense of morality could not be twisted. This beautifully told story will inform you, intrigue you, and generate hope that evil can ultimately be defeated."

Rochelle Dreeben, author of *One Dark Night*

Library of Congress Cataloging-in-Publication Data
Carson-Cardozo, Yvonne
Silence and Secrets: A Jewish Woman's Tale of Escape, Survival and Love in World War II.

Library of Congress Control Number: 2013920636
ISBN: 1493635492
ISBN-13: 978-1493635498

Cover Design: Fiona Jayde
Interior Design: Tamara Cribley
Back cover photograph: Timothy O'Leary
European and world maps: John Plumer
Photo restoration: Jonathan Morgan Jenkins
Interior photographs: Courtesy of Yvonne Carson-Cardozo

1. Memoir. 2. Jews — persecutions. 3. World War, 1939-1945.
4. Refugees — Jewish. 5. Holocaust, Jewish (1939-1945).

Dedication

To my husband George, whom I loved so very much. The thought that I had to continue life without him was very hard on me. When I got married, I believed life together would last forever; but after thirty-three years, George passed away due to illness.

He went through a difficult time during the war, having lost his father in a concentration camp. He couldn't talk about the past either. Marriage changed our lives, and our children gave us a lot of love and affection. I wished we could have shared this book together. My love for him will forever stay in my heart.

To my children, Paul and Vivian, who brought incredible happiness to my life. George and I worked extremely hard so that they would have a better future. They took advantage of the many opportunities and created beautiful lives with wonderful careers. As a proud parent, I couldn't wish for anything better!

TABLE OF CONTENTS

Praise for *Silence and Secrets* . . . . *i*
Dedication iii
Prologue 1
Chapter One: Silence and Secrets 5
Chapter Two: Loss of Innocence 13
Chapter Three: Escape and Survival 17
Chapter Four: At Death's Door 31
Chapter Five: A Bad Mistake 37
Chapter Six: Fleeing France 45
Chapter Seven: Jail or Hotel 55
Chapter Eight: Uprooted Once Again 61
Chapter Nine: Army Life 69
Chapter Ten: Sisterly Reunion 81
Chapter Eleven: Indonesia 87
Chapter Twelve: Returning Home 97
Chapter Thirteen: Finding Love 103
Chapter Fourteen: Starting Over 111
Chapter Fifteen: More Losses 119
Chapter Sixteen: Secret Postcards 123
Chapter Seventeen: Life After George 133
Epilogue: Nevermore 139
Appendices 141
Notes 147
Acknowledgements 149
About the Author 151

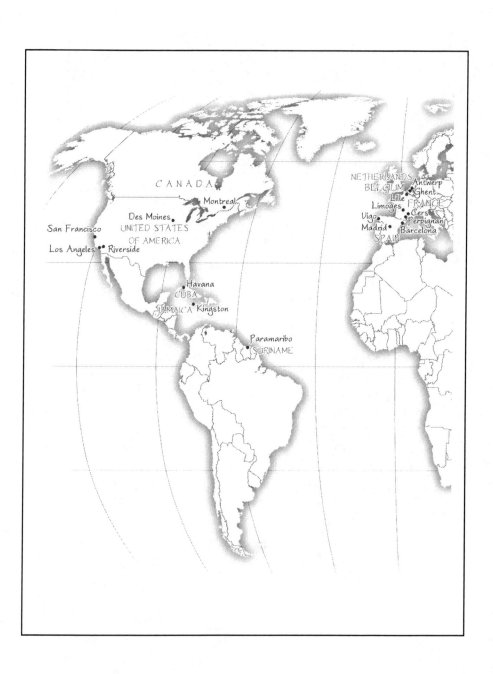

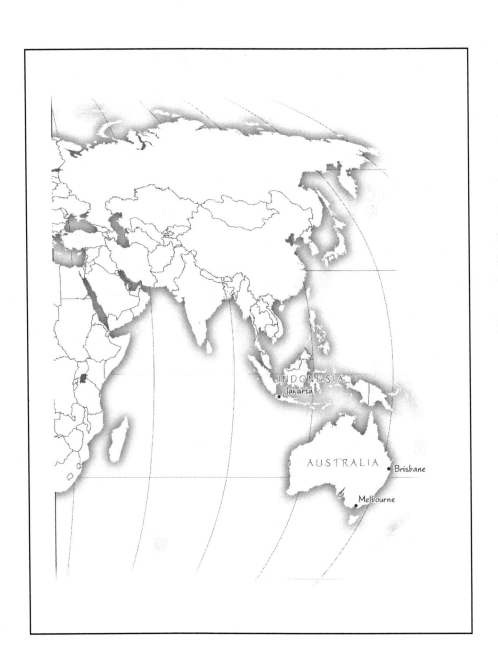

I want to write, but more than that, I want to bring out all kinds of things that lie buried deep in my heart.

- Anne Frank

Prologue

"Shh," whispered Papa. "Don't make a sound. We could be killed. There are German spies everywhere."

I crouched on the straw in the cold, dark barn and trembled at his words. If the farmer caught us, he could turn us in. The thought of being captured by the Nazis made my heart thump and my skin crawl. I had heard horrible stories about them brutalizing people, especially the Jews. I was twelve years old at the time and couldn't understand why anyone would do this to other human beings. Though my parents weren't practicing Jews, I knew I could be killed just for being one. It didn't matter that my family didn't follow the traditional beliefs.

When the Germans invaded the Netherlands and Belgium on May 10, 1940, my parents frantically organized an escape. My mother hurriedly grabbed clothes from our apartment in Ghent as my father went over the plans with my two older sisters, brother, and me. We would dash for the French border, about thirty miles away. Being Jewish, we had no choice but to flee or perish. We left all our precious possessions behind and joined the thousands of frightened refugees choking the roads to escape the onslaught of the Germans.

I had a terribly difficult time understanding this changing world, particularly since I was the youngest of four, and no one took the time to explain much to me. I soon learned that silence and secrets were a way of life: Be quiet; don't tell others.

I peered through the darkness and saw the shadowy shape of my father in the barn. He was not a big man, but always presented himself in a proper way with a keen sense of humor. All that vanished as we hid next to the cows, unsure of our fate. My scared and nervous father, who in the best of times would have joked and reassured me that all was well, made me realize that my comfortable life in Belgium was over. I shivered in the straw, hoping my family wouldn't get caught. Nearby were my sisters, Willy and Mary, who were eighteen and fifteen. They couldn't sleep either. They moved restlessly next to Marcel, my sixteen-year-old brother.

"Be quiet," hissed Mama, frightened that someone would hear. Her clothes were peppered with straw. She was a woman who loved to dress fashionably and display her pretty figure. In the dirty, smelly barn, her fancy clothes and high heels looked out of place, like the rest of us hiding in the hay.

The cows rustled in their stalls, oblivious to any danger. They didn't seem worried about keeping silent. I doubted whether they held any secrets. I wondered how long I would have to hold onto mine.

Over the years, silence and secrecy became an integral part of my life, necessary tools for survival. They began in my childhood, then crept into my relationship with my husband and my children. I didn't want to talk about the past—of escaping cruel Nazis, of joining thousands of refugees fleeing the invasion, of losing my brother who escaped from the train heading for the death camp, only to be caught later, and my many aunts, uncles, and cousins who died in concentration camps.

Though I kept silent over the years, my secrets yearned to see the light of day. Later in life, when I shared my experiences with other people, some of whom were Jewish survivors, I was told, "You must tell your story."

I thought of Anne Frank, a German Jew who spent two years hiding in a secret annex in Amsterdam before being caught and sent to Auschwitz. She was thirteen when she went into hiding in 1942. I was twelve years old when I fled the German occupation in 1940. Many years after the war, I visited the place where Anne once hid and wrote her secrets in a diary. Her words inspired me. She felt compelled to write what was buried in her heart.

At the age of eighty-six, I have finally broken the silence to reveal my secrets from the past, many of which have haunted me since the war. I want to remind others that the Holocaust did occur, and that six million Jews were exterminated. I want to shed light on the fact that millions of refugees fled the violence and sacrificed family, friends, homes, and possessions. The horrors of World War II should cause the world to say, "This will happen nevermore!"

However, even in the midst of evil, I found kindness. Remarkable individuals came forward like angels, holding a light to guide me on the journey. They showed me that kindness does exist, even when people suffer. The compassion of strangers who risked their lives to assist me and my family kept my hope alive that I would not be defeated by evil. Rather, the kindness and caring of others helped me survive so I could finally break the silence and share my secrets.

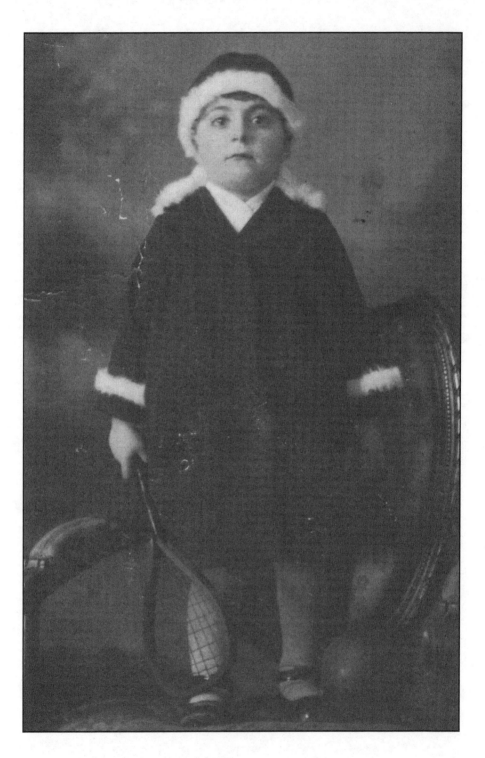

Yvonne at age two, 1929.

Chapter One

SILENCE AND SECRETS

It is not easy to look at the past, but doing so can set you free.

I came into the world as the ugly duckling, or so I thought. Born in Antwerp, Belgium in 1927, as the youngest of four children to Dutch parents, I didn't remember much about my first five years except that my parents often called me the ugly duckling. Since I was the only one in the family with brown hair, my parents would tease me that I wasn't theirs, because everyone else's hair was black. It seemed like a cruel joke. I felt rejected, and questioned whether I actually belonged to the family. It wasn't until after the war, when I obtained a copy of my birth certificate, that I finally believed I was the daughter of Jacob de Leeuwe and Elisabeth van Loon who married in 1921.

Elisabeth van Loon and Jacob de Leeuwe.

I rarely experienced my mother being affectionate. She was the eighth of ten children, and her father died when she was nine years old. I wondered whether that affected her ability to enjoy her children. She would often hit me and my siblings even though we had done nothing wrong. No one was good enough for my mother. As a result, while growing up, I believed I wasn't good enough.

Fortunately, my father enjoyed his children. He treated Wilhelmina, whom we called Willy, as his favorite. She had a great sense of humor, like my father, and, being six years older, she often took care of me. I could always rely on Willy to be there when I was young. Since she loved to play with dolls, she took great pleasure in wheeling me around in a large doll's carriage, showing off her real baby doll to her friends. I enjoyed the attention.

My brother, Marcel, two years younger than Willy, loved to fix things—watches, typewriters, and other mechanical objects. Since he was the only boy, he had his own room, while the three of us girls shared a bedroom. He enjoyed working with his hands and spent more time tinkering than talking. On the other hand, my sisters and mother liked to talk, or argue as was often the case between Mary and my mother, who made it known that she was the boss in the house. Mary played the role of rebel in the family and often fought against my parents' rules.

As a result, I didn't receive much attention from my parents. Thankfully, Willy filled the void by acting as a mother. However, the gap in ages and the continual kidding about my brown hair reinforced the feeling that I was different from the others. I was repeatedly left out of family discussions because their conversations were "not for little ears."

When I was young, I spent a lot of time with Mary since she was three years older. She would often tell me her secrets, with a warning to never tell anyone or else. I quickly learned to keep my mouth shut, lest I get hit.

I remembered a time when my father transported a bubble gum machine in the back seat of the car, between Mary and me. He parked the car for a moment and gave us instructions, "Don't take any bubble gum."

When he left, Mary told me she could make gum appear from her teeth. Unbeknownst to me, she had taken a few pieces. She rubbed her teeth and, sure enough, gum magically appeared. I was so amazed that I couldn't contain myself when my father returned. I shouted, "Mary made gum come out of her teeth!"

Needless to say, my father wasn't happy. Nor was Mary, and if Mary wasn't happy, I would never hear the end of it.

Secrets became part of the family. We never talked about being Jewish. My parents didn't celebrate Passover or other traditions, other than a few Jewish habits like abstaining from pork. We didn't practice the Sabbath, but we kept Friday evenings as a special family night. My mother would serve dishes of goodies — chocolates, nuts, and other sweets. Everyone had to stay home and play games such as Bingo. Since I was the one most interested in playing, I often won. Those Fridays established my love for games.

Since my family didn't practice Judaism, we never talked about the faith in my early years. Consequently, I didn't give much thought to religion. However, I once attended a school with nuns as teachers.

One of my earliest memories is an event that took place in kindergarten. I wet my panties in class and was sent home by an angry nun in a black habit. When my mother took me back to school with fresh clothes, she handed me to the nun. I immediately kicked the woman in the stomach and told Mama later that she deserved it. Needless to say, the nuns wouldn't allow me back in school. I stayed at home with my mother and preoccupied myself with dolls, knitting, and embroidery. I developed a love for handicrafts which kept my mind and hands busy.

When I was five, the family moved to Amsterdam, in the Netherlands, where we lived for the next four years. Three of my mother's brothers and her four sisters and their families all lived in the city. That meant plenty of cousins. My father's four sisters and one brother also lived in the same city, but for whatever reason, I didn't see much of them.

One of the apartments where we lived was within easy walking distance to the shops and schools. Since the Netherlands was a country of canals, one such canal separated the school from the street where my family lived. For one penny, I could take a small boat across the canal. Without that boat ride, I would have had to walk some distance to skirt around the water to get to the school.

My father owned a chemical factory that produced bleach and hair products, like shampoo. When my mother started working with him, a cleaning woman, who happened to be German, was hired to take care of the home. One day, she arrived for work, drunk. She looked at my father and slurred, "Heil Hitler." My papa immediately fired her. He would not put up with such insults.

Though I witnessed the event, I had no idea what it all meant. My parents didn't talk about world events, so I knew little of Hitler, that he had opened Dachau for enemies of the Third Reich in 1933, that he declared himself der Führer of Germany in 1934, or that he stripped Jews of citizenship and most civil rights.

I thought little of the changing world as my family moved to different neighborhoods. I never asked why we left our apartments, and no one told me the reason. Every move meant a new school.

In the third grade, I was enrolled in a Jewish school in The Hague, Netherlands where there was a large Jewish community. In less than a year, I hopped to a new school. When my parents went to Belgium to look for another place to live, my brother, sisters, and I were placed in a Jewish boarding home in Amsterdam. My parents visited us on the weekends, but, again, they never told us why we were there. Silence and secrecy had become the way of our family.

I remembered some fond moments at the boarding house. A rabbi and a cantor living there used to play with me. Each would take a turn and lift me onto his back and carry me through the neighborhood. They were extremely nice and took me to the temple. I felt very important because they paid more attention to me than to the other children. The attention didn't last very long, because my parents collected Mary and me in October of 1937.

Apparently, my father had sold his business and relocated to Ghent, Belgium. Willy and Marcel joined us later, as they were both working at the time in Amsterdam. Since most of my parents' relatives lived in Amsterdam, we left many aunts, uncles, and cousins behind.

I never liked Ghent. There weren't any Jews, and everyone spoke Flemish. I couldn't understand the language and missed being with the extended family. Knitting and handiwork became my salvation. I could do handicrafts anywhere, and they took my mind off problems. I became such an expert at embroidery that I won numerous prizes. One year, I took first place in embroidery at a grand bazaar that included the cities of Antwerp, Brussels, and Ghent. I actually won fifty francs which I quickly spent on a doll and fabric for new clothes and outfits for it.

I learned to sew on my mother's Singer sewing machine by placing phone books on top of the foot pedal that had to be rocked back and forth. With the added height for my feet, my short legs could reach the pedal, which controlled the speed of the machine. I sewed whenever I could and fashioned plenty of clothes for my doll.

As the German armies marched across Europe, my parents began talking more frequently about the worsening situation. My father insisted that war would not come to the Netherlands or Belgium and reassured me that the family was safe. At the time, I believed him, since he, as the parent, must've known what he was talking about. However, when news about the Nazis trickled into the family, I realized how bad it was to be Jewish. I heard horrible stories from Polish, German, and Dutch Jews who arrived at our home, speaking of Nazi beatings and torture. One man had his teeth knocked out while he waited at the German border. I asked how anyone could be so cruel. No one offered a good explanation.

Marcel connected with a rabbi who instructed him in the Jewish religion. He became a strong believer, which was difficult for my parents. They didn't want to be associated with the faith. Clearly, the events taking place in Europe made it dangerous for us.

My father instructed me to tell no one I was Jewish. He asked each of us to call Sal by his full name, Marcel, because it sounded more Flemish. My brother argued that he wanted to be called Sal. Though we were trying to protect him, my brother resisted the name change. We all persisted, and after a while, he came around. The family agreed to keep our background secret. My young mind found the silence and secrecy all too confusing.

The thought of attending school in the new city made me cry the first day on the playground. As it turned out, shortly after arriving in Ghent, I contracted diphtheria. Since I could not stay in school, I was sent with other children who needed medical treatment to a camp in the woods in Dongelberg, near Brussels.

I cried when Mama dropped me off at the train station, feeling abandoned by my family. I didn't even have my doll to comfort me. Was I cursed by my brown hair? Sick and alone, I traveled by train, trying desperately to console myself as best as a ten-year-old could.

When I arrived at the station in Brussels, nuns in black habits directed the children to long tables that had been set up in the middle of the train station. I sat down for lunch and was horrified when bread, butter, and pork were placed in front of me. The other children didn't seem to mind, but I knew my mother had strict rules that bread could not be eaten with ham on it. Hungry, lonely, and scared, I could only cry. A nun came over to find out why I was upset. I told her I wasn't allowed to eat ham. She asked if I was Jewish. I nodded.

She angrily grabbed my sandwich and returned later with two empty slices of bread. I quickly learned another lesson about being Jewish. I would go hungry if I followed the family's rules. Since many of the meals at the camp were pork and beans, I had no choice but to eat the food, like everyone else. I wished my parents would have told me it was all right to eat what I was given.

At the camp, I felt mistreated and desperately wanted my parents to collect me. I wrote them a letter, telling them I hated the place and begged them to pick me up. I handed the letter to the nun, expecting her to mail it. Instead, she read it. Outraged by my words, she tossed the letter into the trash. She made me write another letter filled with lies about feeling better. Again, my voice was silenced.

Nuns closely supervised the children. If any of us mentioned something we didn't like, we would be hushed. Silence and secrets seemed to follow me wherever I went. I cried often and kept my thoughts to myself, hoping to be reunited with my family.

To add to the misery of being ill with diphtheria, I came down with the mumps shortly after I arrived at the camp. Life became unbearable. I lived with horrible sicknesses, prejudiced nuns, loneliness, and pork and beans.

After six horrendous weeks, I was finally allowed a visit by my parents. I promptly begged them to take me home. My father explained that he would arrange my return as soon as he could. I waited three torturous months before I was finally released from the camp that felt more like a prison. On the last day, my mother arrived with my thirteen-year-old sister. After taking one look at Mary, I cried. What had happened to my real sister? Mary had physically developed so much during the past three months that I didn't recognize her.

Feeling rejected, my sister wept along with me. When she brought out my piggy bank accounting book that I had asked her to keep for me, I realized she wasn't an imposter. I welcomed her back into my life with a hug and kiss.

Back in Ghent, I happily rejoined the family. However, world events taking place across Europe caused everyone to worry. The Germans were on the move. My father, as well as many other Belgians, still denied the threat of occupation, believing the country would not be drawn into the conflict.

In the fourth grade, I had an excellent teacher. I enjoyed her classes, particularly when she taught history, which I loved. During one such lesson, she described the end of the First World War when people danced in the streets. After school, I ran home to my mother and told her I wanted a war so I could experience a day of happiness with people dancing in the street when the war ended.

My mother chastised me. "You don't know what you're talking about."

Of course, she was right. I couldn't magically bring on happiness, for people to frolic and dance on the pavement. Not with Hitler and the Nazis marching through Europe.

Amsterdam, 1936.

Yvonne on far right, next to sister, Willy.
Behind them, Mary, and Marcel.

Chapter Two

LOSS OF INNOCENCE

War turns childhood dreams into nightmares.

I was eleven years old when Germany intensified its violent campaign against Jews. The Kristallnacht pogrom, the Night of the Broken Glass, began on November 9, 1938. Nazis terrorized Jewish communities throughout Germany, Austria, and parts of Czechoslovakia. Many homes and synagogues burned, littering the streets with broken glass. Thousands of Jews were taken to concentration camps.

In 1939, Germany occupied the rest of Czechoslovakia and in September, invaded Poland. Tension rippled throughout Europe. I frequently listened to the radio to monitor the news. Most of it involved Hitler's war spreading like a cancer. I wondered if I was safe in Belgium.

When my maternal grandmother died on January 28, 1940 in the Netherlands, my parents decided to attend the funeral. They wanted to pay their respects along with the rest of the extended family in Amsterdam. They realized the danger, so they left Mary, Marcel, and me in the care of Willy who, as the eldest, took on the role of mother.

After taking the train to Amsterdam, my parents met some relatives, then took a taxi to the funeral. The car skidded into an accident. Fortunately, my parents escaped with only minor bruises and scratches. On their return home, they were stopped at the Belgian border by immigration officials. My mother and father had left home in such a rush that they had forgotten their passports. With no proof of citizenship, they were detained by the border guards who believed they were Germans, possibly spies. Thankfully, the guards called the police in Ghent to verify that my parents did, in fact, live in the city. Since we had no telephone, a policeman came knocking at our door. Once he confirmed that we were the De Leeuwe children, he informed us about the car accident. I was horrified at the news and imagined the worst—

that my parents were badly injured, and they wouldn't be allowed to return home.

My sisters, brother, and I were so worried that we waited up all night. We hoped the policeman would convey the information back to the border guards, and that they would release my parents. The wait seemed forever. When my mother and father finally arrived, we met them at the door with hugs of gratitude, relieved that the six of us were back together again.

From then on, I became acutely aware of the pressures of war, not knowing what would happen next. I listened more attentively to the radio for any breaking news. As a child, I still held onto the comforting fact that my parents would protect me should the war arrive at our doorstep. As conflict spread in Europe, however, I became more anxious that Belgium might be occupied.

I was in the sixth grade taking finals when the principal of my school visited each classroom. She showed us a small container that could be an explosive and told us that we could be harmed if we picked up stray things off the ground. I paid close attention to the warning: be careful; it's dangerous times. War was coming. I felt truly scared.

Shortly after that incident, Belgian soldiers occupied the street near my school and closed it down. I became frantic. My knitting was still in the classroom. My handicrafts were my prized possessions. I couldn't bear the thought of losing my knitting. It took my mind off the problems of the day. I told my father that I had to rescue it.

He adamantly refused. "*Je mag niet.* No, you can't."

I protested, "*Jawel, ik kan!* Yes, I can!"

No matter what my father said, I wouldn't listen and continued to protest.

He finally relented and told me, "*Ga snel.* Go quickly."

The soldiers weren't very sympathetic. No matter what I said, they wouldn't let me back into the school. I cried many tears about losing my cherished possession. I didn't realize it them, but it would be the first of many losses.

Since I was no longer in school, I became glued to the radio. War seemed imminent. Sirens were being installed near the school to alert citizens of planes and their bombs. People frantically gathered in the street. Fear was palpable.

On May 10, 1940, I stood in the street with my family and pointed toward the sky. *"Papa, wat is dat?* What is that?"

Before he could answer, the first bomb exploded in Ghent. The sirens, not yet working, sounded no warning. A train nearby took a direct hit. I found out later that the train was filled with the first wave of refugees, along with many Dutch citizens escaping the Nazis. Everyone on board was killed. The Netherlands had been invaded and taken overnight. The Germans were marching into Belgium.

In shock, I stayed on the street with my family. My father talked about returning to the Netherlands, since he was born there, and most of his family resided in Amsterdam. He believed we belonged there. My mother, siblings, and I knew this was a recipe for disaster. We protested vehemently. Why go to Holland when the Germans had already invaded there? Our loud voices outnumbered my father. He finally agreed to escape to France, with England as the ultimate destination.

With images of the exploding train fresh on my mind, I joined the others in the apartment, preparing our escape. The banks were closed, so my father couldn't withdraw money. We had to travel lightly. That meant all important possessions, including our pictures, were left behind. Two prized items that tore at my heart were my knitting and the coupons I collected from Van Nelle tea that could be traded for children's books. The mailman had just brought me a book that I had to leave behind. I forgot about my piggy bank until much later, when I wished for some money.

My dad used whatever funds he had to buy two new bikes, not for riding but for carrying the clothes that were bundled in bed sheets. If we wished to escape quickly, before the Nazis arrived, we could bring only clothes, nothing more.

We painfully walked away from the comfort of our apartment filled with memories. There was little time to say goodbye to friends or neighbors who were frantically deciding whether to stay or leave. Being Jewish, we had no alternative.

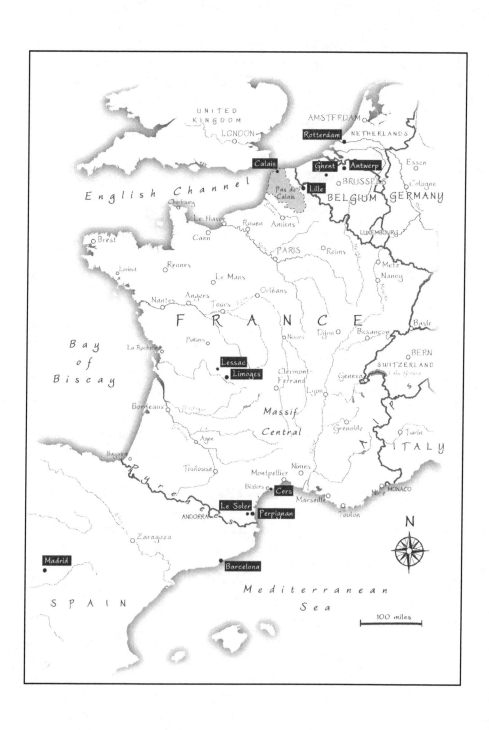

Chapter Three

ESCAPE AND SURVIVAL

Don't get too attached to your possessions.

We immediately fled for the French border, some thirty miles away. Pushing each bike laden with clothes, we joined thousands of refugees escaping from the Germans. Long lines of refugees formed into a human snake slithering along the paved road. Families huddled together in fear, clutching their meager belongings. As the journey progressed and loads felt heavier, people discarded personal items. Unwanted objects littered the sides of the road — suitcases, baby carriages, and clothes. Material possessions seemed unimportant with survival at stake.

I trudged along with my family on the mass exodus. With so many people clogging the road, I kept a slow, steady pace. Though my feet ached, I continued to walk and walk. I never complained. After all, my poor mother was still wearing two-inch heels.

I passed farmland and the occasional town. At times, I talked with strangers. Then again, there were no strangers, for we became one large family traveling a road to safety where religion or nationality didn't play a part.

We would not have survived had it not been for the Red Cross. Along the way, they provided food, mainly pork and beans. As Jews, we never had pork in the house. However, war changed the rules. My father told us to eat what we could to fill our bellies. Those pork and beans tasted mighty good to me. At that time, anything would have quelled my hunger. To this day, the thought of pork and beans makes me think of the war and the Red Cross.

When evening fell, we were on our own to find sleeping accommodations. My family and I slept on straw in smelly barns with snorting horses and rustling cows. The farmers never caught us. If discovered, we hoped they would let us stay. We feared the Germans, who were moving fast. Spies could be anywhere. My dad worried constantly about getting caught. He wanted to protect his family, but the harsh conditions were turning our lives upside down and out of control.

My nights were far from restful. I defended myself as best I could from the fleas, but they, like the Germans, continued their attack. I longed for daylight so I could escape the biting insects. I shuddered at the fate of the Jews who stayed behind in Belgium and Holland to face the wrath of the Nazis.

When my weary feet finally reached the French border, I gratefully stood in line with the horde of refugees seeking to enter the land that promised freedom. Those of us who arrived on foot moved past the border guards much faster than those choking the roads with their cars.

Once we crossed the border, we didn't know where to go. My father had hoped to reach Paris, and then travel onward to England, the grand plan of many refugees. However, French soldiers on horseback directed the flow of refugees through the town of Lille to one road or another. We had no choice but to follow their instructions.

Not used to the constant walking, I tried to hang onto a farmer's carriage when it passed by. Not surprisingly, he didn't let me. My flat feet had always made it difficult to walk long distances. My shoes weren't constructed for such walking, either, so after a while, each step became ever so painful. My only consolation was that I was faring far better than my mother, still wearing her high heels.

I wasn't sure whether it was my father or brother who found a discarded baby carriage on the side of the road, but they decided to put it to good use. Even though I was two months shy of thirteen, I could rest my feet, reclining in the buggy, while family members took turns pushing it some distance. Being small for my age had its advantage. My feet were so grateful. I flashed back to the time when my sister pushed me around in her doll's baby carriage.

After a while, my mother wanted her turn so she could remove her shoes. She sat in the buggy no longer than five minutes when it collapsed. I couldn't help but laugh along with the others at the sight of Mama sitting in a broken carriage in the middle of the street, wearing her finest hat.

My father tossed the buggy to the side of the road with the rest of the discarded possessions. He also decided that the bikes weren't worth keeping and tossed them onto the growing heap of abandoned treasures. He took our bundles of clothes and knocked on a stranger's door. He asked the French family if he could leave our clothes at their home for the Red Cross to pick up later and send to our new address. The family graciously agreed, so he wrote down their address. Our load was much lighter, but we no longer had extra clothes.

Another night meant another stay in a barn. I huddled next to my dad, along with the fleas and flies in the stinky straw. I figured the cows must've been happier because with us there, they had fewer flies and fleas to contend with.

Each day meant more walking, followed by more days of walking. After one such tiring march, I asked the French soldiers if there was a place we could stay for the night. They showed us an abandoned house where other escapees had slept. Compared to a barn, this accommodation was five stars. There were actually beds with sheets. What a luxury! I could finally rest my feet with a good night's sleep and without cows, horses, and fleas.

The next morning my mother scoured the kitchen for something to eat. It felt strange searching another person's home without their knowledge, but it was wartime. I learned the importance of sharing. I straightened my bed and helped the family wash dishes, making everything neat for the next family.

We then returned to walking the road without end, unsure of where we were going. Again, the Red Cross took care of refugees by supplying food — more pork and beans. Without the Red Cross, thousands of people would have starved.

I can't exactly say how, but the six of us ended up on a train to someplace in France. The carriages moved ever so slowly, one mile forward and two back. I remembered a Jewish couple from Brussels who sat nearby. The husband was a jeweler who had placed his valuables in two suitcases. He offered my father one of the suitcases if he and my brother would carry them. My father snapped back with a firm "No," telling the jeweler that everything the family owned was either left in Ghent or on the side of the road. Dad wasn't about to carry someone else's possessions and risk the family's welfare.

The train came to an abrupt stop, not going anywhere. Two well-dressed men arrived onboard, while my father and the jeweler checked a map. The men were clearly German spies who were up to no good. They asked my father where he was taking my family. My father wisely pointed out a different route on the map that we had no intention of following. The men seemed satisfied with the answer and left the carriage. The train started, but when it stopped again, my father quickly ushered us off to safety. I often wondered what happened to the couple from Brussels who remained onboard. They, who had foolishly burdened themselves with treasures, were already prisoners waiting for disaster.

With the Nazis continuing their march into France, tens of thousands of fleeing people jammed the roads. Refugees came from many parts of Europe and spoke different languages. A lot of the Belgians who left their country did so not because of religious persecution, but because they didn't want to fight in the war or end up in a labor camp.

Back on the road, we walked with an endless parade of refugees, wearing our smelly clothes. French police often stopped us to view our passports, which became precious documents. They acted like keys opening doors to freedom. Since my mother's passport contained pictures of Willy, Marcel, Mary, and me, we moved close to her whenever a policeman approached.

I remembered one time when the French police stood everyone in line to check for Nazi infiltrators. One man standing in front of me was a German Jew. A few men overheard him speak German and attacked him, hitting him on the head with a sack containing a bottle. They bloodied his face, but eventually let him go once they realized he wasn't a Nazi. A German passport brought trouble to the owners if they didn't have a good excuse for being in France. With German soldiers on the move, the French police and soldiers handed out harsh treatment to anyone who could be a spy.

Fortunately, Willy knew a little French and became the official translator for the family, as we moved deeper into France. The end of each day brought us to a new place, sometimes a barn, at other times, a house. Though we were exhausted, sleeping was often not possible after a stressful day.

We ended up in Pas-de-Calais, in northern France, where I witnessed death firsthand. Sirens blared to warn everyone to enter the underground shelter. I crawled on my hands and knees between grapevines to enter the bunker where people packed in, standing shoulder to shoulder. I shuddered at the sound of planes dropping bombs, grateful for the surrounding concrete protecting me and the others.

Whenever I felt the earth shake from the exploding bombs, I thought of the farmers who chose to hide with their wives, children, and animals in the large square under the cover of trees, believing they were safe. When the bombing ceased and I left the shelter, I witnessed the bloodshed. Everyone in the square had been killed — mothers with babies in their arms, farmers, and their children. All were slaughtered, including the horses.

That first experience with death and the bloody, grotesque scene has been forever etched in my mind. Some horses were still alive, with their intestines laid out on the square. Soldiers shot them to put them out of their misery.

In Pas-de-Calais, I experienced another fright. My brother had gone missing after we left the shelter. With so many people, getting lost was easy. Marcel accidentally followed others on his way out. My parents wanted to search for him, but the French soldiers ordered us to keep moving. We were not the only ones to lose a loved one, what with all the people on the road.

From that time on, I learned that in order to survive, I had to be strong. No matter if there were corpses, dead cows, burning houses, even a lost brother. There wasn't time to grieve, not if I wanted to escape the Nazis and survive. I couldn't tell when or where the Germans were coming. I only knew that I had to keep walking. Fear became an unwelcome companion. It constantly occupied my mind and body. At that moment, I wondered if I'd ever find my brother.

I learned another important lesson. The prospect of losing someone precious made the discovery all that more joyous. My heart leapt when I spotted Marcel traveling with a group of refugees. I ran to him and hugged him tightly, relieved that the six of us were reunited.

Following the soldiers' directions to travel south, my family and I trekked through the beautiful French cities of Toulouse, Narbonne, and Montpellier. Naturally, safety, not sightseeing, was most pressing. I must have smelled pretty bad, without extra clothes and no place to shower. We had no money, so my family survived with the help of the Red Cross and the kindness of many French people.

I don't know how or why we ended up in the small farming town of Cers, near Béziers in southern France, but it took many days of walking, walking, and more walking. The distance from Pas-de-Calais to Cers measured some 530 miles. My flat feet seemed flatter!

My family ended up staying in Cers for about a year. My weary feet were ever so thankful to be off the road. We lived in a dirty chateau that housed refugees. The large place contained many bedrooms and seemed more like a grimy castle. We were the only Dutch refugees, as well as the only Jews. The other occupants were Belgian farmers who had fled the country after the Germans invaded. My parents would have preferred living with other Dutch people who spoke their native tongue.

A French woman named Lozanne, who was in charge of the refugees in the chateau, lived nearby. She handed out room assignments and arranged for food. My parents, sisters, and I occupied one room, while my brother slept in a hallway. There must've been twenty families living in that house, wedged together like a pack of sardines.

While I had lost the benefits of a normal life, the greatest inconvenience was the lack of a working bathroom. In its place, I had to use the fields. If someone came while I was doing my business, I just moved over. I had gotten used to this during the long walks on the road.

One of us found a white pail with a lid and claimed it as our toilet. My dad hung fabric around it for privacy, if you could call it that. Early in the morning, seven days a week, a little old farmer arrived with his donkey and pushcart to collect the contents of the bucket. The man told me it made good fertilizer for his wine grapes. Luckily, I was deemed too young to empty the pail. That job fell to my brother and older sisters.

Despite the inconveniences, I was glad to be away from the German troops, who had not yet occupied southern France. I truly appreciated a roof over my head, a bed to sleep in, running water, and food in my stomach. All the refugees ate around tables in the large kitchen. I couldn't remember who cooked, but the families seemed to work together. The kitchen served many purposes, including the bathing area where the small children would wash in large pots and pans.

Shortly after we arrived at the chateau, my father contacted the Red Cross and gave them the address of the French family who were holding our clothes. The Red Cross agreed to collect them. Amazingly, the clothes appeared in the bundles just like we left them. That taught me that despite the war, some strangers would go out of their way to help.

Lozanne was another such person. As it so happened, she didn't have any children of her own. She knew I enjoyed knitting, so she brought me wool to give me something to do. What a treat! Lozanne seemed quite happy to spend time with me. She taught me French and helped me with my knitting. Oh, such pleasure to be working with my hands. I so enjoyed my time with Lozanne as she helped me knit a suit. Once started, I couldn't stop. My perfectionist ways kept me on task until I had meticulously completed a new set of clothes.

Having turned thirteen, I was thrilled to wear my burgundy pleated skirt with matching jacket. I strutted around the castle, proudly displaying my outfit. For a moment, I forgot about the war. It had been a long time since I'd felt so happy.

The Belgians eventually left the chateau. Maybe they believed that since they weren't Jews, they could return safely to their homes. I never found out what happened to them. Once they departed, my family occupied the large house. However, we continued to stay in one room, since my dad felt safer having us all together at night. Marcel wanted his own space, so he chose to sleep elsewhere in the chateau.

The castle became deathly quiet without the other refugees. The sound of rats scampering between floors terrified me. I always went to bed first so I could hide under the covers, away from the vile creatures. I once found a little bunny outside and made it my companion—until the rats killed it. I cried over the loss of my cuddly friend.

As if those ugly vermin weren't enough, an infestation of fleas made their home in the quilted blankets on our bed. Before going to sleep, I killed hundreds of them. They multiplied so fast, I gave up the lost battle. Fleas, like the Nazi threat, knew how to torment me and my family.

I wanted to attend school like other children my age. When I asked my father about the idea, he quickly vetoed it. The upper grade levels were held in the city, and I would have to travel by bus or bike. Though I was eager to learn, my dad was more eager to keep me and the rest of the family alive.

"What if the Nazis got closer?" he asked. "If you were too far away from us, I could never get you."

I never stopped being scared. How could I? German soldiers had occupied Paris in June of 1940 and were spreading like rats and fleas. I tried to participate in the conversations about the war, but I was constantly told by my parents that my little ears weren't ready for adult discussions. Silence and secrets followed me, no matter where I lived.

With my mother in charge of the big kitchen, she had to make do with the shortage of food. Lozanne and the French soldiers would occasionally bring us food, but the main menu was turnips. No matter how my mother prepared them, they always tasted the same. I would have been thrilled with pork and beans.

In the fall, the farmers in the nearby village announced the annual grape harvest time or the *vendange,* when the picked grapes would be made into chardonnay. The farmers asked my family if we wanted to participate in the harvest. We all took part. Though we didn't get paid for picking grapes, we were fed wholesome meals with meat. It sure beat turnips and doing nothing. I wondered if the farmers knew we were Jewish. If they did, they showed no animosity and treated us very well.

While picking grapes off vines was enjoyable for me, it didn't agree with my mother. I did half of her work, picking my row of grapes and circling around to complete her section. My small body was limber and healthy, so I didn't get a sore back like my mother did.

The farmers enjoyed our contribution so much that they made a song and sang it to my family: *Les Français sont gentils et les Hollandais aussi.* Translated, it meant: The French are nice and so are the Dutch. At the end of the *vendange,* the farmers' wives cooked a hearty meal, which was always welcome. They served plenty of wine, but since my father wasn't a drinker and didn't want to offend the farmers, he would quietly move his glass of wine to Marcel. My seventeen-year-old brother happily obliged.

My two sisters had turned nineteen and sixteen and quickly made friends in the village. They met a few French soldiers, who were more than happy to spend time with them. They told Willy and Mary to visit them after dinner and to bring some pots for the leftovers. The wonderful food meant we didn't go to bed on empty stomachs.

Cers, France, 1940.

Parents standing behind Willy, Marcel, Mary, and Yvonne at thirteen.

One day, a Dutch priest from the city heard about us and stopped by for a visit. My parents were ecstatic because they had an opportunity to speak their language. The priest stayed for a few hours. He must've taken a liking to me because he said, "Little girl, next time I will bring something for you."

Though I was thirteen, I looked much younger. On his next visit, he remembered his promise. He handed me a child's toy — a monkey on a string. I was mortified. I couldn't insult the priest, so I graciously accepted his gift.

My brother had great fun at my expense. Marcel slapped the wooden monkey on the wall, making annoying sounds to tease and irritate me. I was really mad at him but couldn't say anything, not with the priest there.

The following year, the same priest visited our new refugee home and evidently learned my true age. He seemed embarrassed, as he probably remembered the monkey. Needless to say, I happily lost the toy.

One day, the Dutch Consul, Mr. Kolkman, brought his wife to have breakfast in Cers. When he learned that a Dutch family lived nearby, he appeared on our doorstep with his wife in hand. After meeting my parents, he told them that a new refugee home was opening near Perpignan, fifty miles away. He asked if my father would be interested in taking over as the director of the facility. He could supervise the running of the house and my mother could work in the kitchen. The opportunity sounded fantastic. Not only would we be residing with other Dutch refugees, but the Dutch Consulate would be nearby, in Perpignan. It didn't take much convincing for my father to say yes.

The move would take us farther south, where we would be safer from the German soldiers. They had not occupied the southern zone when France surrendered on June 20, 1940. The Vichy Government was formed under the rule of Marshal Pétain. He established a fascist regime that collaborated with the Germans. Though he maintained control over the unoccupied southern part of France, he followed the instructions of the Nazis.

Mr. Kolkman arranged for train tickets and, after one year in Cers, my family took to the road again. Though we remained ever alert for soldiers and police, the trip proved uneventful as we made our way to our next home.

Located near the Pyrénées Mountains, in the district of Le Soler in southern France, the refugee home in Perpignan, *maison Mazard,* was another mansion with many rooms, but only one toilet. It stopped working soon after we arrived, and everyone returned to the fields whenever nature called.

We found the home already populated with some twenty families with young children. Fortunately for my sisters, some of the boys were similar in age. Unfortunately, none of them was turning fourteen, like me. I had hoped one of the boys would have shown some interest. To my disappointment, I was ignored. However, my sisters enjoyed the attention and had plenty of friends.

Marcel kept himself busy as Mr. Fix-it. When we left Belgium, he had placed a few small tools in his pockets. He put those screwdrivers and pliers to good use. He loved taking things apart and putting them back together again. He eagerly worked on watches and other mechanical items that needed repair.

To occupy my time, I watched the men play chess. One young man, who stuttered, gladly showed me how to play. He turned out to be a good teacher, and I learned fast. Soon, others recognized my talent and eagerly competed with me. My social life picked up, because of a game.

Living with a large group of people in the best of times presented logistical problems. Factor in the shortage of food, cramped conditions, lack of amenities, fear of the Nazis, boredom, and personality clashes, there were bound to be arguments. One of the main sources of conflict was food, because turnips became the main course for breakfast, lunch, and dinner. My mother valiantly tried different recipes, but in the end, turnips still tasted like turnips. Once in a while, we received a small piece of bread, and if we were really lucky, a piece of cheese.

My parents sat the children at different tables so no one would think they were served more food than the others. Sometimes a parent would act deceitfully to get additional rations. One mother complained constantly about her sick nineteen-year-old son. He looked fine to me, but the mother pleaded for more food to keep him from getting ill. Her embarrassed son would kick her under the table to stop her from talking. Sadly, she often got her way, and that meant less rations for the rest of us.

My father realized the hopelessness of living in France. Young men were being forced by the French Vichy regime to provide free labor for the government. Marcel had to work with others to build a bridge in Le Soler. They labored hard, without much food. When the bridge was finished, it collapsed, not surprisingly, since the workers had little experience constructing bridges.

Seeking help, my father wrote to Queen Wilhelmina when we were living in Cers. He asked for her assistance with passage for the six of us to Indonesia. After the Germans occupied the Netherlands, Queen Wilhelmina fled to England where she took charge of the Dutch government while in exile. Since Indonesia was still part of the Netherlands, the Queen could intervene on our behalf.

Miraculously, my father received a letter from the Queen herself. She wrote that affidavits and tickets would be sent for us to take a ship to Indonesia. The family rejoiced at the prospect of sailing away from the Nazis and the misery of living as refugees. We anxiously waited for the papers, but they never arrived. Little did we know that they were sent to the Dutch Consulate in Perpignan. We discovered much later that the tickets were given by the consulate to six boys who lived in our refugee house.

I had already learned that life was unfair, but still, the disappointment hurt. The promise of a better life had instilled some hope to keep going. As that hope faded, so did my health.

In order to survive, you have to be strong.

Some refugees at maison Mazard, southern France, 1941.

First row, from right to left –
Yvonne, Father, Willy, Mother, and Mary.

Chapter Four

AT DEATH'S DOOR

In the worst of times, you can find kindness to ease the pain.

By 1942, two years had passed since we had escaped from Belgium. Life at the refugee house near Perpignan deteriorated. Sanitation became a serious problem. The nearby stream became so polluted that I could smell the foul stench from the window. Rats occupied the surrounding area and became unwanted house visitors.

The unsanitary conditions, plus the shortage of food took its toll. Willy and I became weak and seriously ill. Marcel also wasn't feeling well, so he joined us on the visit to the village doctor, who seemed fresh out of college. Whether he lacked interest or experience, he said there was nothing wrong and sent us home with one instruction: take long walks early in the morning. When we followed his recommendation, we merely got sicker.

Mr. Kolkman from the Dutch Consulate became so concerned about us spreading the illness to the other refugees that he took Willy to the hospital in Perpignan for a second opinion. After examining my sister, the doctor kept her in the hospital for four days. He also asked to see me, since I suffered from the same condition.

Worried that I wouldn't survive if he drove me to the hospital, Mr. Kolkman ordered an ambulance to transport my skinny, sick body. I must've weighed no more than a hundred pounds. When the ambulance arrived, the drivers brought in the stretcher. I became frightened that the entire village would gawk at me. I refused to get on the stretcher and mustered my strength, telling the drivers, "No way."

They reasoned with me. They would allow me to walk outside if I promised to lie down on the stretcher in the ambulance. That I could live with, not that I really had much choice. As I suspected, the villagers waited around to find out who was ill. The ambulance became a village event.

Adding to the drama, the drivers wanted to take my mother after they heard she was in bed with the mumps. Dad told them he wanted her to remain at the house and promised to look after her. Losing two daughters to the hospital was bad enough. He didn't have other family members to spare.

My sister, Mary, and her boyfriend didn't want to pass up the opportunity for a free ride in the ambulance, so they talked the drivers into letting them come along. I appreciated the company and hoped I'd be able to see Willy at the hospital.

I was blessed to be under the care of a French doctor who happened to be the director of the hospital. He was one of the kindest men I met during the war. He placed me on the adult ward next to my sister's bed, which was against hospital rules. I was fourteen at the time and, though nurses and patients complained that I should be in the children's ward, the doctor was adamant. "The two sisters must stay together."

He told me later that my sister and I were so sick that he didn't think we would survive. Our skin had turned yellow, and we could hardly walk. We suffered from hepatitis and typhoid fever.

I found the large, open ward extremely difficult. It contained twenty-five or thirty beds with patients having a range of physical and mental illnesses. There was no privacy, without any curtains around the bed. However, being next to my big sister proved to be the best medicine. I could talk to her about my fears and worries. During those three to four months in the hospital, I forged a stronger bond with Willy. She told me later that she appreciated the closeness.

My sister and I began our agonizing recovery as a result of the doctor's excellent treatment and genuine kindness. Contrary to the one in the village, this physician truly cared for our welfare. He went out of his way to ensure that we received the best medical help. I felt safe in the hospital and well cared for by him and the staff.

During that time, my brother, then eighteen, had a severe bicycle accident. With most men in the army, Marcel was one of the few young men available to work. He carried an assortment of tools and eagerly fixed mechanical problems. He was often sought after, and even worked for the local police department.

On one of his errands, Marcel crashed on his old bike when the front fork snapped. He smashed onto the road and fell unconscious. Miraculously, the accident occurred in front of the house of my doctor, who happened to be at home. He provided emergency treatment to Marcel's bloody, lacerated face. While administering bandages in his house, the doctor asked my brother's name.

"De Leeuwe."

"Do you have two sisters in the hospital?" asked the physician.

Marcel nodded.

The amazed doctor then told him that he should come up with a good excuse for not visiting us. He didn't want me or Willy subjected to any more stress, as our bodies were very frail. Seeing my brother's bandaged face would have created more strain and worry.

Following the doctor's instructions, my parents told us during a hospital visit that Marcel was too busy to drop by. Only after he had healed did he show his face. A scar was still present on the last picture taken of him.

After two months in the hospital, the doctor told my parents that Willy and I needed to regain our strength because we were so weak that neither of us could stand. He suggested that the family relocate because of the health risk in the current house. The unsanitary conditions were so bad that the health department had visited the refugee home, yet took no action.

Since there were severe restrictions about traveling, my parents went to the consulate of the Netherlands in Perpignan, where Mr. Kolkman gave the approval for my parents to move to another refugee home in Lessac, not far from Limoges, in central France. My parents packed our belongings and took Mary and Marcel with them one month before Willy and I were released from the hospital.

Before they left, my parents bought a large bar of chocolate, which they acquired on the black market. Willy and I both loved dark chocolate. However, we were instructed by the medical staff not to eat our favorite treat. My sister and I clung to one another for support, desperate to recuperate and rejoin our family, but we needed that bar of chocolate to ease our pain.

On one of his visits, the doctor found Willy's nightstand drawer open. He spotted the chocolate and asked us where it came from. We confessed that our parents left it as a gift. He firmly told us, "No chocolate. It must be returned to your parents."

After he left, we decided to pretend that his instructions were meant for the next day. We giggled and ate the whole lot. Dark chocolate never tasted so good.

I still don't know why I didn't get sick, because I hadn't eaten solid food in months. In addition to the intravenous fluids, I was fed milk four times a day. No one had milk unless prescribed by the doctor. Once, a heavyset patient on our ward yelled out, "Nurse, nurse, I want milk just like the two, two…"

I held my breath, believing she would say, "Two Jewish girls."

Instead, she muttered, "Dutch girls."

After that incident, I became frightened that she knew we were Jews. I avoided any contact with her because she could have caused trouble. Oddly enough, one year later, she became responsible for saving our lives.

I suspected that the doctor and some of the patients and nurses knew who we were. They didn't ask us; we didn't tell. Harboring Jews could bring serious problems. The secrecy and silence kept everyone safe.

As we recovered, my sister and I were allowed visitors from the refugee home, which was quite a distance from the hospital. I thought the boys who arrived came to see Willy and me; however, I soon realized they were interested only in my attractive twenty-year-old sister. Some French boys cleverly listed us as their family so they could drop in, as well. Willy loved the attention, and I enjoyed the company.

Once we were able to walk again, the doctor issued a pass so we could leave the hospital for a few hours and stretch our legs. We visited a Belgian family that my mother had met on a previous visit to the hospital. They lived on the same dead-end street as the medical facility and often invited my mother to their apartment. They were extremely nice to her, since we had lived in Belgium, and even dropped by the ward to visit Willy and me. On our brief jaunts away from the hospital, we stopped by their apartment. We really had nowhere else to go, and they seemed genuinely happy to see us.

When my sister and I were finally released from the hospital, we were still weak. We bid our farewells, thanking everyone for their wonderful care, especially the kind and compassionate French doctor. Anxious to rejoin our family, we boarded a train in Perpignan for the 230-mile trip to Limoges. Even though we felt safe with the doctor's discharge papers in our purses, we could never be sure about the French police or the German spies. We kept a close watch, hoping that the six of us would once again be reunited.

Limoge refugee house, 1942.

Chapter Five

A BAD MISTAKE

Some mistakes lead to unexpected outcomes.

I exited the train, happy to see my parents on the platform. Willy and I ran to them and showered them with hugs. As usual, my father was more emotional than my mother, who tended to be more reserved. Dad immediately handed me two hard-boiled eggs, figuring I needed something to eat. In my excitement, I squashed one of them in my hand. I didn't care, because I was once more with my family.

Since there was no transportation to take us to the new refugee home, La Partoucie in Lessac, we had to walk several miles. I couldn't bear the thought of walking, especially since I had not fully recovered from hepatitis and typhoid fever. Feeling weak, I put on a brave front and said little, hobbling along as best I could.

As luck would have it, a farmer was passing by in his horse-drawn carriage. When he offered us a ride, my feet rejoiced. I didn't care that the journey took forever; but it was far better than trudging along on foot.

My parents had originally asked to be sent to the refugee home in Toulouse where they had friends, but the place was already packed. In wartime, we learned to take what we could get, and sometimes we were blessed for it. I found out after the war that my future husband, George, and his parents stayed in that house in Toulouse. George had left the place to fight in the *Maquis,* the underground resistance which blew up railroad lines, harassed Nazis, and disrupted the war effort. His father was eventually deported from the home to a concentration camp. If my family had lived in Toulouse, we might have found ourselves on a convoy to the death camps. Survival during wartime often resulted from strange twists of fate.

The refugee home in Lessac turned out to be an old, overcrowded mansion filled mostly with Dutch Jews. The fact that few had possessions, including basic amenities like toothbrushes, made it easier to occupy the house. No one had to worry about storing their belongings or carting suitcases and furniture.

Unfortunately, like the previous house, there was no bathroom. Going to the toilet by the bushes had become natural. If I ran into another person while squatting, I'd pick up my underwear and shift to another spot. In such overcrowded conditions I stopped feeling embarrassed.

On one of my father's visits to the bushes, searching for his private spot, he discovered two chicken eggs. He returned to the house quite excited at the prospect of fresh eggs for breakfast. He took one egg and left the other one for the hen, hoping she would return to the same place and lay some more, which she did.

With the scarcity of food, I really enjoyed those cooked eggs. Sadly, the supply didn't last very long. Either someone discovered our secret or the chicken was killed, yet another casualty of the war.

Cooped up in the crowded mansion with little to do, everyone talked about the war, and if they survived, what they would do. The radio kept us somewhat informed of the events in 1942. With Germany bombing England and battling the Russians, there appeared to be no end in sight. I wondered if I would remain a refugee forever.

Tension rippled throughout the mansion. With food and space being scarce, the adults argued constantly about everything, but mostly about food. I left the adults to their bickering, not wanting to take part in it. The last thing I needed in my life was more stress. Instead of enjoying my life as a fifteen-year-old, I worried constantly. Would the Germans occupy southern France and capture us? Would I get out of this war alive? Would I get sick again? Would my family survive?

No one in the house knew what was really going on in the world, and with so much time on my hands, I felt like a poor lost soul. I was locked out of the world with little to do.

During those bleak times, a shining light appeared in the presence of a kind Italian, named Sisto. A tall, good-looking young man, Sisto lived with his family on a farm nearby. He formed a close friendship with Willy, who had become an attractive twenty-one-year-old woman. We all adored Sisto, who seemed like one of the family. I never thought he and my sister became romantically involved, but if they ever had, there would have been complications. Sisto's parents were against the relationship because Willy was Jewish, and she had no intention of being a farmer's wife. No matter, because Sisto treated Willy and the rest of us as if we were his own. If we needed food, he helped out. If we needed medicine from the doctor, Sisto found a way to obtain it. This kind Italian became one person our family trusted with our lives.

Shortly after moving to Lessac, Marcel talked about escaping from France. He had befriended two other boys in the refugee house. Even though one of them was mentally handicapped, Marcel wanted to take the boy with him. The three boys talked about climbing the mountains and entering Switzerland.

My parents were heartbroken at the thought of losing their nineteen-year-old son, and tried to talk him out of his daring escape. My brother was adamant; he wanted freedom. Eventually, my parents gave their blessing, believing that if he could escape, at least one member of the family would taste freedom.

Before he left, I showered my brother with hugs, not knowing whether I'd ever see him again. He and his friends then departed Lessac and headed for the Swiss border. A rabbi in Perpignan provided them with money for a guide. The one they hired agreed to take them to Switzerland on the condition that they carry the luggage for a Jewish couple and their two children. I doubted whether I would have agreed to those terms, but Marcel and his friends were anxious to flee.

They journeyed over the mountains and after much difficulty, arrived at the Swiss border. The customs officials informed them that no one could enter unless they had proper papers and money. Marcel and his companions had Dutch passports, but no money. Since the couple had both, they were allowed to enter, whereas my brother and his friends were instructed to leave immediately or be handed over to the Nazis. So much for Swiss neutrality!

At the time, I had no way of knowing whether Marcel made it to Switzerland. I kept imagining that he escaped. His departure made my parents realize that the conditions in the refugee house were deteriorating, with little food and rising tension. They decided it was better to go into hiding. Our trusted friend, Sisto, again came to our aid. He made arrangements to collect us in the middle of the night and take us to a farmhouse where a farmer, living alone, would shelter us.

One dark evening, my family and I disappeared from the refugee home, not telling a soul. Without silence and secrets, it would have been impossible for five people simply to vanish without anyone in a crowded mansion noticing. But vanish, we did. Only our trusted Italian knew of our whereabouts.

Shortly after we went into hiding, Sisto brought a surprise — my brother. I hugged him, rejoicing that our family of six had been reunited. Marcel then shared his journey. He told us about the failed escape to Switzerland, about returning to the refugee house and finding us missing, and about looking for Sisto, knowing we would have confided in him.

While I was happy to have my brother back, I felt deeply disappointed that he hadn't escaped. If Marcel couldn't find a way to leave France and the Nazi threat, how could the rest of us? I wondered if I, myself, could endure such a difficult journey. Hiding, however, offered no guarantee of safety, as my family soon discovered. A gas man arrived one morning to check the farmer's meter. Terrified of being spotted, everyone quickly hid. After that incident, my parents decided that after ten days at the farmhouse, we should return to the mansion in Lessac.

When we arrived back at the refugee house, the police were notified. The refugees, believing something horrible had happened to us, had called the French police. Fortunately, the authorities didn't cause any problems; however, the refugees treated us quite differently thereafter. They were probably frightened about our vanishing and reappearing act. After all, Jews were vanishing every day in Europe.

My family returned to the very same room and the unbearable conditions that we had left. Marcel immediately formulated another escape plan for himself. He found a woman who said she was with the underground. She told him she would do whatever she could to help him get to England. There, he would work in the secret service. She brought paperwork for my parents to sign and make it official. My father realized he couldn't stop Marcel, so he signed the papers. My brother was convinced this was the best plan for him to get out alive. Having failed on his first attempt, he desperately wanted to escape the deteriorating situation with the growing threat of the Nazis.

Marcel left, never to be seen again.

Shortly after his departure, every refugee in the house received a ration card and was ordered to wear the yellow Star of David. The six-pointed star, with the French word *Juif,* had to be displayed prominently on the clothes. My dad became so angry that he tore up our cards and ripped the stars. He refused to demean himself.

I was terrified of what would happen if we were caught not wearing the identification badge. The Vichy government cooperated with the Germans and could easily round up Jews for slaughter.

I began talking with Willy about our own escape plan. We had discussed it numerous times, but were reluctant to tell our parents, who wanted to keep the family together. We finally told them of our desire to escape to Spain. At first, they were shocked. However, considering the gravity of the situation, escaping was a far better plan than remaining there, to be found and butchered.

Willy and I reviewed our strategy with my father. We planned to find a guide who would help us over the mountains. We realized that moving to Lessac from Perpignan was a mistake. Had we stayed at our old refugee home, we would have been near the Pyrénées Mountains and the Spanish border.

We went over different options in case we were stopped by the Germans. Sisto would help us travel from Lessac to the Limoges train station. From there, we would take the train to Perpignan and look for a guide. We promised our parents that we would write them using a code, since mail was heavily censored. We had to be careful about what we put in the letter, so we would keep it brief and seemingly ordinary, telling them, "The package arrived." That meant that we were safe. During the war, others used the same code.

We felt it was better for Mary to stay with our parents. Willy and I worked well together, and we worried that Mary might reveal our plans, since she tended to talk a lot. She seemed content to stay behind with our mother and father.

Once again, two in the family had to disappear from the home. Willy and I nervously grabbed our bags and, with Sisto's help, headed for the station. To avoid suspicion, my parents told the other refugees that we were going to stay with friends in Limoges. I wondered what the refugees really thought.

Not surprisingly, the train was packed. We stood during the entire six-hour trip, deciding not to sleep, so we could keep watch for any police or soldiers. Concerned about the authorities discovering us, we planned to go to the restroom together if we spotted any officials. We kept silent most of the way, so no one would hear our Dutch accents.

While the train rumbled along, I noticed Willy nod off while standing. She dropped her purse to the floor, spilling her belongings. I nervously avoided the passengers' gazes and stooped to collect the purse and its contents. From then on, Willy and I helped each other stay awake for the rest of the trip. We were exhausted, so it was amazing that we both stayed on our feet.

When we reached Perpignan in the afternoon, we went straight to our Belgian friends whom we had met on numerous occasions while we were in the hospital. We hoped they could help us. Willy and I apprehensively crept past the hospital. We had stayed there three to four months, so knew the nurses and staff would remember us. Nevertheless, we took the risk that we wouldn't be spotted.

We approached the dead-end street that housed both the hospital and our Belgian friends. Suddenly, I heard someone call out our names. The doctor who treated us yelled from his car and honked his horn.

At fifteen, I had developed into a teenager, so I hoped he wouldn't recognize me. I pretended not to pay attention, wishing he would go away.

"Hey!" he shouted, honking his horn again.

We couldn't ignore him anymore. We stopped to say hello. He must've seen that we were terrified of getting caught, because he immediately said, "You should know I won't report you."

He acted as nice as before, telling us he was glad to see us and that we had recovered and looked so well. Without his medical care, Willy and I might not have survived. I later regretted not asking him for help. He could have guided us to shelter. Then again, he had already put himself in danger by treating us. He was truly a wonderful man. Sadly, that was the last time I saw him.

Since we decided not to involve him, we continued with our original plans. I nervously approached the apartment. After hearing my knock, the Belgian mother opened the door. Spotting us, she looked terrified. She grabbed our arms and led us straight to her bedroom. She told us that her daughter married a Spaniard who could not be trusted. He would be arriving shortly, so we had to stay in the bedroom and remain absolutely quiet. Not a peep.

My body reacted like it usually did whenever I got scared. I had to go to the bathroom. In that situation, I couldn't relieve myself, not with the son-in-law about to arrive. When he came, I sat on the bed for several hours, not making a sound. I couldn't even whisper to Willy. The pain became unbearable. I wondered what would happen if the Spaniard entered our room.

By the time he finally left, I could barely contain myself. I had to go so badly. However, the mother opened the front door and demanded that we leave immediately. She didn't offer food, guidance, or the chance to visit the bathroom. She wanted us gone. I understood how dangerous it was to hide us, so I couldn't hold it against her.

Willy and I quickly searched for a toilet. Since our best-laid plans had fallen apart, we wandered the streets of Perpignan, unsure about our next step.

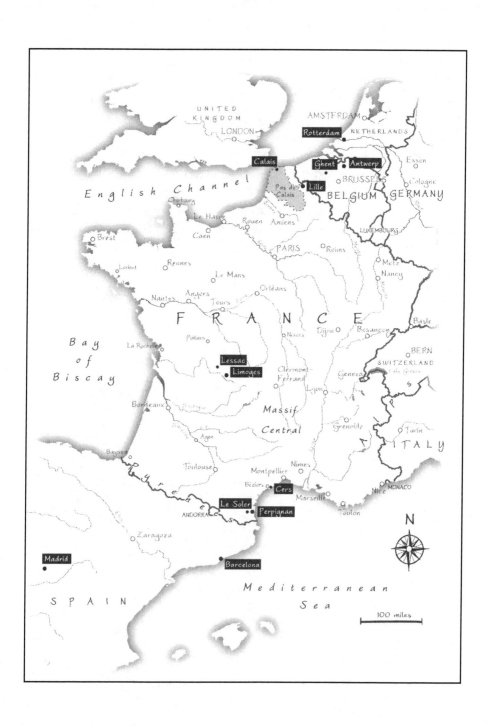

Chapter Six

FLEEING FRANCE

Horrible acts can force you to find courage.

We kept out of sight of any police, knowing we had to find a safe place before evening. We could only think of the Red Cross. We hurried to their office before they closed and hoped they would help.

I crossed my fingers as I walked in the room. When I spotted the heavyset woman behind the desk, I panicked. I had met her before, in the hospital a year ago. She was the one who complained to the nurses about Willy and me receiving milk, crying out, "I want milk just like the...Dutch girls." I knew she meant to say, "Jewish girls."

Willy and I froze. Had we made a horrendous mistake by coming to the Red Cross?

The woman sensed our fear.

"Don't be afraid," she said. "I have changed. I'm here to help you."

Her words brought immediate comfort. She asked us what we needed. We disclosed our plans to cross the Pyrénées Mountains to enter Spain. She listened patiently, then told us to wait while she talked to a person in the back office.

That started a remarkable chain of events for which I am forever grateful. Upon her return, she guided us to a small room where she introduced us to a fifty-year old French lady, dressed in a dark suit, who worked with the underground. The heavyset woman wished us luck and departed. The kind and courageous action by that stranger, who risked her life, eventually led to our freedom. I never had the chance to thank her for saving me and, no doubt, countless others. During war, horrible acts were committed, but so were generous, brave deeds.

The lady from the underground contributed with her own courageous part. After questioning us about our plans, and after hearing about Marcel and his failed attempt to enter Switzerland, she agreed to help us escape with our parents and sister. But first, we needed a place to spend the night.

When it was dark, she guided us through numerous back streets to an old house. I felt scared about not knowing where I was or who I was actually with. After using the downstairs toilet, a hole in the ground, I followed Willy and the woman upstairs to the attic. The bare room contained a double bed and a small, dim light in the background to prevent anyone from viewing us from the outside.

We were instructed not to leave the room or make any noise, under any circumstances. She told us that she'd be back in the morning to collect us. I wondered who else might be in the dark house, but never heard a sound. My mind whirled with fear. Were others hiding? What if she didn't return? What if she intended to hand us over to the Nazis? As usual, when I became frightened, I had to visit the bathroom, but the lady said, "Don't leave the room."

I stayed put and held on until the morning.

In desperate need of a decent night's sleep, I drifted off, feeling quite proud of our accomplishments. Willy and I had made contact with the underground, and they were prepared to help us escape.

Thankfully, the lady arrived in the morning. I quickly walked down four flights of stairs to visit the toilet. I must've been exhausted the previous night, because I never remembered so many steps.

The lady told us that the five of us in the family needed French passports. They would be made by people in the underground, but we needed photos. Once we had the pictures, and the family was together, she would connect us with a guide who would take us over the mountains to Spain. More information would be given when we were ready to leave.

There was one major problem. We had to let our parents know that we needed passport pictures and that we had organized an escape plan. With the mail heavily censored, one of us had to return to Limoges. I became the unlucky one. Since I looked younger than my fifteen years, I was the logical choice. If the Germans ever entered the train, I planned to fool them by pointing at a couple as if they were my parents. That probably wasn't the best of plans, but it was the only choice I felt I had.

Willy went with me to the station and kept me company. Before leaving on the evening train, I nervously headed to the toilet. My sister was concerned about me and became my lookout to make sure I would be safe until I boarded. Traveling late meant another sleepless night. I kept an eye on the passengers who entered the train during each stop. When a couple of men who looked German came on board, I immediately went to the bathroom. Once the train started moving, I returned to my seat, but remained ever vigilant.

Because I would be sitting at least six hours on the train, I chose an aisle seat in case I had to leave quickly to hide again. I kept to myself and pretended to sleep, opening my eyes periodically to check the passengers. It was easier to fit into the crowd, since it was late evening. Most people were trying to rest. Even then, anyone could be watching me, so I remained alert, especially since I didn't have any identification. Luckily, no German soldiers or French police boarded that night.

I departed the train in Limoges and hurriedly ran from the station to the home of Dutch Jews who were friends of my parents. I needed a place to refresh myself after traveling without food, water, or sleep. They were surprised to see me alone, but they already knew that my family had a way of coming and going. I was grateful they didn't ask many questions — not that I would have said anything. My brief respite with them took my mind off the shock of the past few days and the anxiety of the upcoming journey.

I was thoroughly exhausted, but didn't take them up on their offer to spend the night. I couldn't waste time sleeping. I wanted to see my family. Luckily, a farmer on the road offered me a ride in his hay-filled wagon. The horses trotted faster than I could ever walk the long distance to Lessac and the refugee house. Seated in the wagon, I relaxed enough to chat casually with the farmer during the ride.

When I reached the house, I rushed inside to surprise my parents. After a round of hugs, I quickly explained that Willy was fine and remained in Perpignan, where she would wait for us to join her. My parents had a million questions, but I needed sleep. With little strength to offer the details, I collapsed on the bed and slept soundly, knowing that my parents were nearby. That bed never felt so good.

In the morning, I told Mary and my parents all that had happened. They were amazed that we not only contacted the underground, but also would obtain new passports as soon as we supplied photos. We immediately made arrangements for individual pictures to be taken in Lessac and sent to a secure address given by the underground in Perpignan. Once they had our photos, they would make French passports and personally deliver them.

After a couple of weeks, we received a letter from Willy telling us to expect a package. That was our secret code, meaning that the lady from the underground would soon arrive. When she appeared, she brought a passport for each of us — my father, my mother, Mary, and me. She gave further instructions about the escape plan before she departed.

With all the preparations complete, my father enlisted the aid of Sisto. The Italian young man never ceased to amaze us with his loyalty. He found a farmer who would be delivering his sacks of flour to Limoges, where we would catch the train. This, hopefully, would be my family's final escape. No doubt, the remaining refugees in the house were left with something to talk about.

I didn't know where my father collected the money, but he paid the farmer to take us in the middle of the night. Dad took a leap of faith to trust yet another stranger. Along the way, the farmer was stopped by the French police. When questioned by an officer, he pointed to the flour and told him he was making a delivery. I was petrified the police would search behind the sacks where we were hiding, and felt the urge to empty my bladder. After being frightened so often, I would have thought I had better control over my bodily functions. As I had done in the past, I desperately held on. Luck was on our side. The officer let the farmer pass.

In Limoges, we were let out in the dark so we could make our way to the station. If it wasn't for that man and our loyal friend Sisto, who risked their lives for us, I wouldn't be sharing this story. Many people came forward during a time of need to help us reach safety. However, the journey was far from over.

Since we knew French, Mary and I moved to the counter to purchase the tickets. We had instructed my parents not to talk in Dutch, because if the police asked them about their French passports, and they couldn't speak French, we would surely be picked up. I suggested they pretend they were deaf and mute. This fell by the wayside when Dad noticed French police approaching the spot where Mary and I were buying the tickets. He nervously called out in a loud Dutch voice, *"Mary en Yvonne, kom hier!"*

I froze at my father's words. We had hardly started our journey when he veered from the plan. I checked the police. Apparently, they didn't hear him, or they decided to turn a blind eye, for they didn't intervene.

Intermingled with the many people who were traveling that night, we made it safely onto the train with no one asking to see our papers. I told my parents that the best thing they could do was to sleep while Mary and I kept watch. I spent another fitful night over the six-hour train ride. Oh, to have a few good nights' rest!

We arrived in Perpignan early in the morning. Willy waited for us at the station, along with the French lady from the underground. It had been previously arranged for me to approach Willy and kiss her on the cheek, as if we hadn't seen each other in awhile. If no one intervened, Mary and my parents would follow us, keeping a short distance behind. We didn't want to walk as a group of six, which could easily attract attention.

Some officials checked people's documents on the street, but thankfully, they never stopped us. We walked briskly for several blocks, then disappeared into an old house where we hurried to an upstairs apartment. Not a moment too soon.

"Shush," said the French lady. She called us to the window. "Look! The *razzia* patrol."

The whole street had been blocked off for the *razzia* to patrol the streets and look for Jews or members of the resistance. I shuddered at the thought of the police squad finding us, now that my family had been reunited. Someone must have reported us.

We all breathed a sigh of relief when the patrol finally left. The woman with the French resistance then laid out the escape plan. We would leave Perpignan by bus, where we would find a guide to take us over the Pyrénées Mountains into Spain. We were to look for an older man who would signal us with his head. If the bus ever stopped for the police, the man would nod his head, meaning, stay on the bus. If he shook his head no, we were meant to get off the bus.

We began our journey on February 6, 1943. We boarded the bus that would take us to the mountains. I wore a heavy, green wool coat that my mother had constructed from another coat. Although it was short, it would block the cold wind from the mountains. I had only one pair of shoes, leather flats, for climbing.

I expected to recognize our guide, but since there were several older men on the bus, my family and I were unsure who to follow. I kept checking all the men for any sign of a nod or shake of the head. A slightly heavy, gray-haired man who dressed like a farmer sat across from us. Was he the one?

The driver stopped to take on more passengers. The French police stepped on board to check everyone's passports. When they moved down the aisle, I frantically scanned the older men, looking for a sign. The gray-haired man sitting across from me nodded. He was the one. His signal told us to stay on the bus. The police viewed our documents without a word, then left. After that frightening incident, no one in the family said anything for the rest of the trip.

When the driver pulled over for our stop, the old man shook his head, signaling that we should leave. He joined us and six French boys by the side of the road. Once the bus drove on, the guide properly introduced himself to my family and the six boys who, to my surprise, were also planning to leave France. Eleven of us would be making our way on the great escape.

We walked toward a young man waiting with a donkey and cart to transport our packages. We had none, so the donkey got off easy that day. Since leaving Belgium, we had learned to travel light.

Our guide led us to what looked like a large barn. It turned out to be his home. Inside, we sat on the floor by candlelight while his wife served us supper, something I never expected. How I cherished that beautiful meal and the quiet, precious time with my family, the French lads, the guide, and his wife. I ate in silence, not knowing whether that meal would be my last.

When it was pitch black outside, the elderly man told us we would be taken to a rendezvous point in the mountains. There, we would wait for ten minutes, or until his replacement arrived to escort us into Spain. He then asked us to repeat an oath that we would stay together as a group, no matter what, and that we would take care of each other at all times. That oath strengthened our bond as a group. We would either escape together or perish together.

I was comforted by the presence of the six French boys, who were all under twenty. Since they had taken the same oath, I figured they could help out in case of an emergency. Little did I realize they would end up saving my life.

I repeated the oath like a mantra, over and over in my mind, as our group followed the guide. He shined a small flashlight on the path, but even with the light, it was difficult to see. Nonetheless, I trudged along the trail, longing to be free of Nazis and German spies. After an hour and a half, we reached the rendezvous point where our guide bid his farewell. His replacement would lead us the rest of the way. We offered the kind man bountiful thanks for helping us regain our freedom.

After he left us in total darkness, I kept my fingers crossed that the next guide would show up. There was no way we could find our way through the mountains at night. However, survival had become engrained in my way of life, so I repeated the oath, hoping that everything would work out.

As promised, the replacement arrived on time with his flashlight. The terrain up and across the mountain proved difficult, especially for my mother who was still wearing her only shoes, with wooden soles and two-inch heels. Though it was winter, the path was dry, with some trees dotting the landscape. I shuddered at the thought of trekking through snow and mud. We climbed rocks and zigzagged up and down the Pyrénées. Sometimes, the path was wide, while other sections were narrow, with a few treacherous ledges along the way. The long journey was terrifying. Not only did I have to cross a massive chain of mountains in the dark without water or food, but I was constantly in fear that we might get caught by the Germans and their guard dogs.

We stopped periodically to gather our strength, but the pace was slow. Fatigue set in, but I had learned not to complain. At one point, the guide turned off his flashlight and warned us that Germans might be nearby with their sniffing dogs. We silently crept along the mountain pass in total darkness, with nothing to illuminate the path.

It had been a long, strenuous day with little sleep. I felt exhausted, but still trudged on. The path narrowed, and I stepped gingerly without any light to guide my way. Suddenly, I screamed, unaware of what was happening. I lost consciousness.

When the fog lifted, I opened my eyes. I became alarmed that my parents and sisters were crying. The six boys and our guide quietly huddled nearby. I heard someone tell me I had fallen asleep and wandered off the ledge of the cliff. I had tumbled downward, heading for the rocks. Luckily, an overhanging branch speared the inside of my green woolen coat and caught me before I could plummet to death. Apparently, my screaming, as I dangled from the tree, saved my life. The group might not otherwise have noticed that I had disappeared into the blackness below. Fortunately, the Germans were not around, for they would have heard my loud screams and captured us. Once the French boys located me, they formed a human chain to pull me to safety. They clearly followed the oath that we stay together as a group and take care of each other.

I put on a brave front because my parents and sisters were still weeping. I pretended that I was all right, though I knew the severe pain in my right foot, leg, and back indicated something was seriously wrong. Regardless, I had to keep on walking. There was no turning back.

That harrowing experience woke me and the others up. Each of us stepped more carefully on the mountainside. I limped onward, walking and climbing. I blocked out the pain to keep pace with the others.

As the sun began to rise, we reached a vista. Our guide pointed to the nearest village. Spain was in sight. He wished us luck and bid his farewell. We thanked him for being yet another kind person who risked his life for no other gain than the satisfaction of helping others reach freedom.

The eleven of us were on our own. We were a sorry sight of exhausted travelers heading toward the village. My mother, looking worse for wear, lost any desire to maintain a proper appearance. After the long, tiring climb, her fashion sense fell apart as her flat, blue hat slipped down to the side of her face. This caused everyone to burst into laughter, creating comic relief from the tension of the treacherous climb. My mother forced a smile and adjusted her hat and two-inch heels. We were ready for Spain.

Make the time to thank others for acts of kindness because you may not have another chance.

Madrid, Spain, 1943.

Left to right – Yvonne, Father, Mother, Willy, and Mary.

Chapter Seven

JAIL OR HOTEL

Appreciate the simple pleasures of life, like indoor plumbing.

My father told the six French boys to continue on, because our family couldn't keep up with their young legs. Remembering their oath, they initially refused to leave, but we finally convinced them to carry on without us. No sense holding them back. I was exhausted and coping with the excruciating pain in my back and right foot, which felt broken. Nonetheless, I hated to say goodbye. They had rescued me from the fall. I never had the chance to thank them properly. Though I knew the boys only a short time, they had become like family.

I pushed myself forward, despite the horrible pains, and climbed downhill. After a while, my mother stopped at a village that occupied three levels on the mountainside. She couldn't walk anymore. Actually, neither could I, but I didn't want to say anything. My father suggested that he and Willy walk ahead to find the best way to get down to the first level of the village. He would scout around and return as soon as possible.

From a distance, I watched them walk into the village and come to an abrupt halt. What had they spotted? They kept staring at a little shop. Apparently, they were gawking at a fruit store with huge, sumptuous oranges, something they hadn't seen, let alone tasted, in years. There was fresh fruit!

Apparently, one of the villagers alerted the police across the street about the two strangers in town. I saw my dad talk to an officer and point toward us. Another policeman came to collect my mother, Mary, and me. We joined my father and Willy at the police station. So much for freedom!

Since none of us knew Spanish, it was difficult to communicate. Fortunately, one policeman spoke a little French and conversed with Willy. She asked him what they were going to do with us. The officer said he was taking the five of us to Figueres tomorrow to be shot.

Upon hearing that, I froze, believing I had just survived the mountains only to face a firing squad.

My father immediately asked the police to put us in jail. He knew that Spain still maintained a diplomatic link with the Dutch government, and that there was a consulate in Madrid. Other refugees had told us that if we ever made it to Spain and were incarcerated, we should contact the consulate. My father asked the police to do just that.

After a long conversation with the Dutch authorities in Madrid, the police informed us that we'd be taken to a hotel, under their supervision. I realized then, my life would be spared. The officer was obviously kidding. But I wasn't laughing. After thirty-three terrifying months as a refugee, I would never joke about killing someone.

The police escorted my family and me to a hotel. I was expecting a shabby building, so was shocked when we entered a lovely hotel. We were assigned a room with soft, white sheets on the beds. What luxury! We ate in the hotel restaurant where we were treated to a wonderful meal on a white tablecloth, paid for by the Dutch government. I had forgotten about the niceties of life, especially after the refugee houses with turnips as the only food. For the first time in ages, I felt like a normal human being.

Though my family was under house arrest, with an officer standing guard outside our door, I couldn't have cared less. I felt safe in a place with good food — and toilets. At that moment, I almost forgot about my injuries from the fall.

The following day, three policemen took us by bus to another village. Along the way, they picked up the six French boys who had traveled across the mountains. They had walked deeper into the country, only to be arrested. We were all happy to see each other. I felt like we had been reunited as one big family.

When we arrived at the village, the officers accompanied my family to a nice hotel across the street from the police station. Sadly, the boys ended up in jail. My sisters and I visited them when we could and brought food. They truly deserved their freedom, but there was nothing we could do. I thought they would be freed like us, but being French, the Spanish police treated them differently.

A representative of the Dutch Consulate arrived at the hotel and treated us exceptionally well. From that point on, we were in their hands. Not only did they put us up in a fine hotel, but they gave us clothing and spending money. What a treat to wear new clothes!

While I felt well looked after, the one thing I really cared about was my long-awaited freedom. I often wondered about my brother, and talked about him to my parents and sisters. I wanted to believe he had escaped, like us, to a safe place. His absence left a gaping hole in the family.

Bearing a letter from the Dutch Consulate, we moved twice more by bus, first to a hotel in Barcelona for four days, then to Madrid. Many Dutch people were staying in a hotel, but since that accommodation was full, the five of us were rewarded with the bridal suite in another hotel. I had gone from living in a rat-infested house without indoor toilets to a luxurious suite with a comfortable bed and clean sheets and a beautiful bathroom. Back then, I learned to appreciate the simple pleasures, like indoor plumbing.

I didn't tell my parents about the ongoing pain in my back and right leg and foot, but limping gave it away. I was taken to a doctor who spoke only Spanish. During the examination, I couldn't understand him, but soon discerned that my right foot was broken, and a bone in my leg was cracked. My neck and spine weren't in good shape, either. At any rate, I was grateful to be alive after falling off the cliff.

Surviving taught me to endure pain. I hobbled along without a cast or crutches. I did, however, receive physical therapy from a forty-year old man who taught classes at a gym, or what would now be called a health club. I would arrive an hour before the exercise class, and he would treat my foot, leg, and back with massage, exercise, and stretching. He did an amazing job putting me back together.

As my body healed, I felt the tremendous emotional relief of no longer living in constant fear of the Nazis. While in Madrid, I made up for those lost years in France. I turned sixteen, still too young to date according to my parents' standards, but they allowed me out of the house with my sisters. The three of us found boyfriends and stayed up late. I so enjoyed the vibrant, lively city, filled with interesting people. I visited museums, drank coffee in the cafés, and made friends. I loved the siesta naps. They made up for all those lost hours of sleep.

In 1943, the war still raged between the Axis countries of Germany, Italy, and Japan and, seemingly, the rest of the world. I felt lucky to be safe, with a roof over my head, food in my stomach, and no need to hide. While I knew my family couldn't stay in Madrid forever, I soaked up the happiness during those five to six months. Part of me knew it wouldn't last.

Sometimes to survive, you have to endure pain.

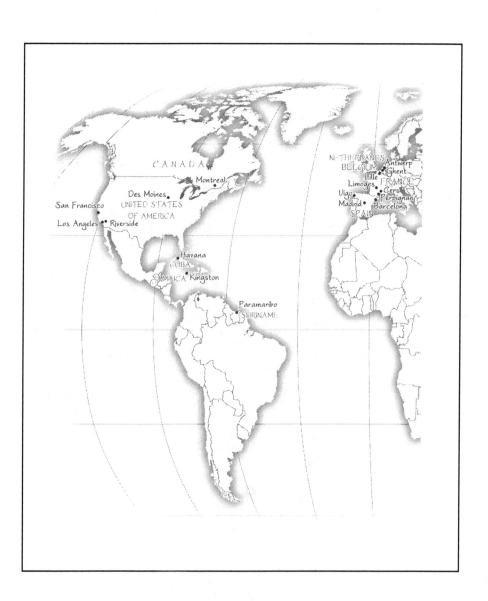

Chapter Eight

UPROOTED ONCE AGAIN

Life is unpredictable, so expect the unexpected.

When the consulate informed my family that we were being sent to Jamaica, I was deeply disappointed. The Spanish lifestyle had grown on me. However, the truth of the matter was that we were still refugees and had to go where we were told. Saying farewell had become part of my life.

In August 1943, my family joined the other Dutch passengers at the port of Vigo where we departed on the Spanish ship, *Marqués de Comillas*, a former luxury liner. The overcrowded ship was packed so tightly, the Spaniards must've cleared out the two hotels in Madrid that housed the Dutch refugees. Our family of five squeezed into one cabin. The ship headed to Kingston, Jamaica. Since this was my first voyage, I acted like an excited teenager. Surprisingly, the food onboard was quite good—no turnips—and the service wasn't bad, either. I wondered what it would be like in another country some 4,300 miles away.

Marques De Comillas ship, 1943.
Left to right – Yvonne, Willy, Mother, Father, and Mary.

Yvonne heading for Jamaica.

While I enjoyed life on the ship, I never felt completely out of danger. With the ongoing war, the captain warned us that German submarines could attack the ship, even though it carried civilian passengers. Blackout nights were common, with lights extinguished and drapes covering each window. During those critical times, passengers weren't allowed to sleep in the cabins. Couples and single men slept on the deck while the women were quartered in the lounge. Without any light, I had to feel my way around for an empty couch or cushion to sleep on.

If I wanted to shower, I could do so in the cabin, but only in the morning, then had to return promptly to the deck. Despite the inconveniences, I was pleased to be in the hands of a trusted captain. My faith proved right, for we arrived in Jamaica without any interference from the Germans.

One lesson that I had learned over and over again was to expect the unexpected. In Jamaica, while waiting in line to collect my luggage, I was suddenly removed by a thirty-year-old female official, acting very businesslike. She escorted me to a separate building, then into a small room. She ordered me to take off all my clothes and didn't say why. Being naked in front of a stranger terrified me. She ended up strip-searching me and inserting a flashlight. I felt scared to death. Never had I endured such humiliation. I wondered if my sisters received the same treatment, or if it had happened only to me. I kept silent and held onto that secret.

Years later, I told my mother about this incident. She said she'd heard about such things, but didn't know I was strip-searched. Apparently, the previous refugee group had smuggled in diamonds or gold. I asked her why she didn't talk to her daughters about it. I received her typical reply, "In those days, we didn't talk about that sort of thing."

Clearly, silence and secrets were reinforced by my mother.

Every refugee was assigned to barracks that looked more like a prison camp. Women and children were housed on one side, with men on the other side of the camp. Barbed wire surrounded each building. Each day, refugees were collected for mandatory interviews. After being questioned, the person was assigned a new home. Since my family had been placed at the end of the list, we were last to be interviewed.

Living quarters had been erected for refugees. Inside each barrack, the wooden partitions were open at the top, making privacy impossible. For meals, we would stand in line to collect our food, then sit outside on benches alongside tables. Showers and tents and, once again, stinky outhouses had to be shared. I was so scared of the gigantic cockroaches that I would grab a large rock and throw it at the insects to scatter them. I would then relieve myself as quickly as possible. I hated close, personal experiences with those creepy creatures, but they were better than the Nazis.

Jamaica was a far cry from the luxurious conveniences of Spain. Freedom seemed to vanish behind the barbed wire. There wasn't much to do, but now that I had blossomed as a sixteen-year-old, one of the Finnish boys showed an interest in me. I felt very important and grown up. Though I was shy, talking seemed to be the best way to pass the time, even though we communicated in broken English.

After several months, we were ordered to leave Jamaica for Dutch Guiana, a small country now called the Republic of Suriname, located on the northeast coast of South America, that shared a southern border with Brazil. We sailed on the Dutch ship, the *SS Cottica,* about 1,700 miles toward the port of Paramaribo, the capital city. I enjoyed that trip because we were on a Dutch vessel, and the crew spoke the same language. They were exceptionally friendly and threw a few parties. We celebrated New Year's Eve of 1944 the Dutch way, with a night of eating and partying.

Since we were traveling on the ocean, the captain, like the one on the other ship, ordered occasional blackouts to prevent German attacks. We were sailing far from Europe, so we were in safer waters. However, the captain wanted to ensure our safety and took all precautions.

When we arrived in Paramaribo, everyone was locked up again, but thankfully, only overnight. The Dutch government had built small, two-bedroom homes for the refugees. Willy and Mary shared one room and my parents the other, while I slept on a cot in the empty kitchen. I didn't mind the basic accommodations, but I hated using the stinky outhouses. In addition to the cockroaches, there were now rats and snakes.

At night, I had to watch where I walked whenever I went to the dining room, located in another building. I avoided stepping straight down from the curb because rats and small snakes often stayed there. As far as I was concerned, those creatures could keep their hiding place. I happily jumped over them.

At that time, Dutch Guiana was still part of the Netherlands, so the official language was Dutch. I expected to stay there for the rest of the war.

"Not so," said my dad. He was scared of the disease elephantiasis, which was transmitted by mosquitoes. The unfortunate people infected with the ugly disease had badly swollen and disfigured parts of their bodies. Since many women in Paramaribo had contracted elephantiasis, my father didn't want to risk his four women catching the disease.

He knew some Belgians who had escaped the invasion and migrated to Cuba, where they worked in the diamond business. He contacted an old friend there and asked if he could find a sponsor for us. When he was younger, my father had worked with diamonds in Antwerp, the diamond capital of the world. Experienced people in the industry were always in demand. Luckily, someone from Cuba sponsored him.

After living in Suriname for three months, I said farewell yet again and joined my family on another move, this time on a seaplane. The craft took off from the water, and after flying some 2,100 miles, landed in Antilla, Cuba. We ferried to Customs, only to discover that it had closed for the night.

My family and I had to wait to be processed, so we stayed overnight in a little house built on stilts in the ocean. Inside were beds and rows of rocking chairs. The mosquitoes swarmed and attacked like German planes. Another sleepless night. I rocked myself silly to give the hungry mosquitoes a more difficult moving target. I consoled myself that at least I was safe, unlike the countless refugees in Europe suffering in concentration camps, starving, and fearing for their lives.

The next day, my family cleared customs, and we connected with my father's friend in Havana. We stayed a few nights in one hotel, then moved to the Sevilla Biltmore. Our hotel room contained a small kitchen so my mother could, once again, cook her traditional Dutch dishes of chicken soup and baked fish.

I fell in love with Havana. The Cubans seemed full of life. Singing and dancing could be found twenty-four hours a day. My parents chose to live in Havana's downtown area, close to President Batista's palace. I figured what was good for the president was good enough for my family.

Though I was seventeen, my sisters and I often spent time together, even with the differences of ages — Willy at twenty-three and Mary at twenty. We met a Jewish Cuban couple who brought us to the beach. Though I swam in the sparkling blue warm water, I preferred to spend time socializing with others.

The three of us dated as a group, each with our own male companion. We visited downtown Havana, where music and dancing flourished. Though the war raged on in Europe and the Pacific in 1944, I enjoyed the good life in Cuba.

Since I had time on my hands, I decided to make some money by painting lampshades with Disney characters for children's rooms. My favorites were Mickey and Minnie Mouse and Pluto. Willy helped me with my daring business venture and accompanied me to a few stores, where I negotiated with the owners to supply me with white lamps. I would paint Disney characters on them and sell the finished product back to the owners. I felt so proud whenever my lamp shades sold, because no one knew I had taught myself to paint.

Getting the business off the ground in a hotel room wasn't easy. The *camarero,* or hotel steward, was instructed not to clean the top of the armoire where I kept my collection of lamps. However, I eventually stopped making them because they took up so much room. I switched to belts because they didn't require a lot of storage space. I designed the belts and hired a shoemaker to manufacture them. I painted figures of oriental men and women on the leather. I also created jewelry boxes made of glass and ribbon. I'd sell the belts and boxes to small boutiques. The business kept me quite busy, though I made sure I had time for friends.

Since my father worked in the diamond business, I asked him if I could learn the trade of diamond cutting. It seemed a perfect fit for my love of handicrafts. After he helped me find a job at the diamond factory, I gave up my business and applied myself to diamonds, supposedly a woman's best friend.

By 1944, many people had relocated to Cuba from the Netherlands. When the Dutch Consul threw a cocktail party for the Dutch residents in Havana, my family and I received an invitation. Even though I was unsure of the purpose of the occasion, I wasn't about to turn it down. After all, a party was a party. I didn't have to travel very far, because the banquet room was downstairs in the hotel where my family stayed. It made it easier to drop in and enjoy the cocktails and hors d'oeuvres.

With everyone in a festive mood, the Consul addressed the crowd. He appealed to the single women in the audience to enlist in The Royal Netherlands Indies Army. At that time Indonesia, which still belonged to the Netherlands, had been seized by the Japanese. The Dutch military needed women to help after the anticipated liberation of Indonesia. With few places to recruit soldiers, the Dutch government sought women who were living in foreign countries. Since there weren't many available Dutch girls in Cuba, my sisters and I decided to sign up right there on the spot.

Caught off guard, my parents were shocked at the prospect of losing their three daughters. My sisters were adults and I was seventeen, so they had little say over our decision to enlist. My sisters and I wanted to do our part in the war effort.

Willy and Mary were immediately accepted. As I was not yet eighteen, the Dutch Indonesian Army considered me too young.

I was very disappointed at not being able to join my sisters. They departed shortly thereafter for basic training in Denver, Colorado.

Left alone for the first time with my parents, I returned to my life in the hotel and at work. Having made a number of friends, I became part of a group that enjoyed going out together. If I worked additional hours on the weekends in the diamond factory, my friends would stop by and sing a song as a signal to come out and socialize.

After a while, I no longer felt the need to join my sisters. Since I was having so much fun, why join the army? My attitude changed when I received an official letter from Washington, D.C., with my name on it. Fortunately, I was at home during the mail delivery because my parents might never have shown it to me. The letter informed me that my name had been included on the list to join the army. After reading the message, I had to go.

I was still underage, at seventeen, and wondered if I would be the youngest member of the WAC, Women's Army Corps. I didn't care, as long as I could eventually join my sisters and support the war effort. Willy and Mary were nearly done with their basic training.

When it was time to leave Cuba, my friends and parents escorted me to the airport. It was difficult leaving them behind, but I was ready for my new life in the army. I received so many presents from my friends that when I went through Customs, the officials removed many of them from my suitcase. However, as soon as the gifts were removed, my friends somehow managed to stuff them back in.

My parents later told me they thought I was going to cry at the farewell. I had learned to survive in life, so I put on a brave front and boarded the plane with a smile on my face. I was ready for the army. I wondered if the army was ready for me.

Yvonne at army training in Des Moines, Iowa, 1945.

Chapter Nine

ARMY LIFE

The unknown may be scary. Overcoming the fear makes you stronger and gives you amazing stories to tell your children.

When I arrived in Miami, I expected to be picked up by an official from the Dutch Consulate. Not finding anyone, I grabbed a seat at the airport and hoped they didn't forget me. Eventually, I spotted a little boy walking around with a sign that read, "De Leeuwe." I announced myself to the youngster, who then asked me to follow him to the information desk where someone was waiting to speak with me on the phone. I was surprised to talk with the consul himself. He told me that he had been paging me on the intercom. Since my name had been mispronounced, I didn't realize he was trying to contact me. He apologized for not collecting me in person. He would inform the information desk to organize a taxi to drive me to a hotel where I could enjoy the rest of the day. The army would pay for my accommodation and meals. I wasn't about to argue with those arrangements.

I checked into a lovely hotel, then spent my first stay in the United States touring Miami. To ensure that I wouldn't get lost, I kept a card with the hotel's address in my purse as I wandered around the neighborhood, visiting beaches and shops. Since I had attended a Berlitz School before leaving Cuba, I knew enough English to get around. By then, I could speak Dutch, Flemish, French, Spanish, and English.

After dinner, the consul arrived and drove me to the train station. He handed me an official letter with my orders. He then bought me a first-class ticket. New experiences continued to present themselves as I traveled on a sleeper train. I had never heard of, let alone slept in, a sleeping berth. Before retiring, I took advantage of my first-class status and visited the bar. Since I was underage, I couldn't order liquor, but then again, I was shy, so I kept to myself. Still wearing street clothes, I admired the soldiers dressed in their uniforms. Soon, I would be one of them.

I was originally supposed to travel to New York, but my new orders directed me to travel to Washington, D.C., before moving on to basic training in Des Moines, Iowa. As it turned out, the train was delayed four hours. When I arrived at the station, Sergeant Veder greeted me, after waiting in the middle of the night. Apparently, he had known me when I lived in Suriname and easily spotted me. He and his family were Dutch refugees, but I didn't remember him.

The sergeant treated me exceptionally well. He brought me home to stay with his family. His wife woke up when I arrived and showed me to the bed that had been made up in the living room. She also remembered me from Suriname, but I still couldn't place her or her husband.

The next morning, when their two boys greeted me, I instantly recognized them, because I had socialized more with the children in the refugee camp than with the adults. The family made me feel at home and gave me a royal tour of Washington that included the White House.

That evening, the sergeant took me to the train station. I continued my journey to Fort Des Moines, a military training camp for women. Thus began my life in the army.

I arrived on April 15, 1945 after eleven in the evening at the small train station in Des Moines, Iowa. I had expected someone to greet me, but since no one came forward, I found a bench and waited and waited. Eventually, the station-master asked me why I had not left, because the station would close at midnight.

At seventeen, I had already learned to be remarkably independent. I was well versed in solving problems, even tiny difficulties, so I showed him the official letter that clearly stated I would be picked up at the station. He called the military base, and they confirmed that, indeed, they had forgotten about me and would drive to the station immediately.

Two female sergeants arrived and escorted me to the base. Because everyone was asleep, they couldn't turn on the lights in the barracks. At two in the morning, they guided me to a bathroom so I could prepare for bed. They mentioned that four Dutch girls were nearby, a comforting thought. What they didn't tell me was that at five in the morning, someone would blow a whistle, and I would have only fifteen minutes to prepare for the day.

After the tiring day of travel, I fell fast asleep. I had a comforting dream about returning home and meeting my parents. The next thing I knew, the lights went on, with girls running around, yelling, "Quick, get ready. It's inspection day."

They scurried around, all the while asking me where I came from. Still in a daze like a zombie, I could hardly get dressed. Fortunately, someone made my bed. By the time the major walked in, everyone was dressed in striped outfits that had been issued for the first two weeks. Since I wasn't in uniform, I easily stood out.

The major checked around, then approached me. He gave me a push. "You're new."

He didn't have to tell me that because I, along with the others, already knew that.

During breakfast, I became acquainted with the four Dutch girls, who ranged in age from twenty to forty. They couldn't understand how I entered the army, since I looked much younger than my seventeen years. I told them I was a reject since I was so young, but they desperately needed the Dutch.

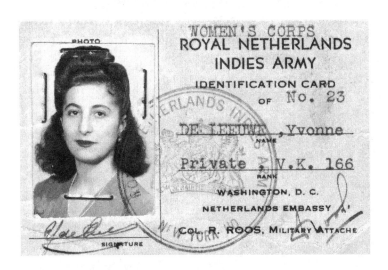

Royal Netherlands ID card, 1945.

Basic training began immediately in Company 13, 3rd Regiment, First Women's Army Corps Training Center. I spent many days studying in the classroom with plenty of marching on the side, singing, "Fall in, fall out; fall out, fall in; that's all we ever do!"

We followed the military code of perfection, with shoes polished, uniforms crisp, and postures erect. I was born a perfectionist, so I didn't mind that part of the army. To this day, I still make sure my made-up bed has no wrinkles.

When I received my uniform, I looked and felt much better. Dutch soldiers were issued khaki uniforms like the Americans, except the caps and jackets carried the insignia of the Dutch Lion. The Americans thought the insignias meant we were officers and, therefore, saluted us. We Dutch girls obligingly saluted back. We had so much fun playing the role of officers.

I quickly developed a close relationship with a twenty-two-year-old girl named Boudina. Coincidentally, she had two sisters in the army who were stationed with my two sisters. Though she came from a very different background, having been raised by Dutch parents in Vancouver, Canada, Boudina became my best friend and confidante. She hardly spoke Dutch, and I was still learning English; however, language never became a barrier. We quickly bonded and became inseparable. The confined quarters, the shared experiences in the army, and the continued support of a friend helped me for the first time in my life to break the silence and reveal my secrets about the harrowing escape to France and my ongoing journey to survive.

Having a close friend like Boudina made the six weeks of basic training less painful. When studying military history, I had to expand my English very quickly. Fortunately, the tests were multiple choice, and I did fairly well. If I wasn't in class, I was marching. And if I wasn't marching, I was standing on the parade grounds for hours at a time. Since I'd had plenty of practice walking across France and climbing the Pyrénées Mountains, the marching came easy.

Kitchen duty was my least favorite. During my stretch in the army, periodically I had to wash the dishes and clean the oversized pots, which were so big, I could have easily fit into one. During my last stint of kitchen duty, I threw up when I inhaled the greasy stench. The female sergeant wasn't sympathetic. She didn't have to clean up the mess. However, one of my friends felt sorry for me and asked for and received permission to take my duty. I was ordered straight to bed — one of the best orders I had ever received.

On May 7, 1945, Germany surrendered, and on May 8, the war in Europe was declared over. The Nazis had been defeated. While I was grateful for the demise of the German army and the liberation of Europe, there was plenty of work to do. The war with Japan continued and soldiers were still needed to protect people in the countries that had been occupied. Eventually, I would be sent to Indonesia once the Japanese were defeated.

I completed basic training in early June of 1945. When it was almost over, I received the horrible news that anyone going overseas had to complete an additional six weeks of training. The Dutch government tried to intervene, so the Dutch soldiers could miss those extra weeks, but since the American government provided the training, they wouldn't budge. Rules were rules.

The next six weeks were grueling. I learned to use a gas mask; handle and shoot a rifle; crawl through mud with my pack and weapon; and exercise muscles I never knew existed. In the end, the difficult training prepared me well.

Full gear, army training.

When the extra training was finally complete, the five of us Dutch girls received our new uniforms. We exchanged khaki for navy blue. The Dutch Lion emblem that we wore on the left shoulder of our old uniforms was transferred to our new blue ones. We looked very much like officers, and the American soldiers continued to salute us as such. I proudly saluted them back as Private Yvonne de Leeuwe.

Des Moines, Iowa, 1945.

Left to right – Johonna, Boudina, Yvonne, Sanna and Sophia.

During this time, Boudina and I met a few boys who asked us out. We gladly accepted. The day before our date, we immaculately made our beds, tidied the quarters, and lined up our polished shoes. We didn't want to end up on the demerit list, which was posted in every barrack. When anything was out of line or done incorrectly, punishment would follow, which meant extra work.

Boudina and I were getting ready for a fun night when we reviewed the new list. To our surprise, black marks had been placed next to our bed numbers. We couldn't understand how that was even possible, because we had double-checked everything.

For punishment, we had to mow the lawns, and, sadly, skip the dates. We were fuming!

The next day I learned that a mistake had been made, and the wrong list had been placed in our barracks. To add insult to injury, neither Boudina nor I ever received an apology. I had already learned that life could be unfair.

Then again, life granted occasional favors. On the night when Boudina and I finally went out with our dates, we were running terribly late. We would surely get in trouble if we arrived after curfew. Boudina told me that she knew of a shortcut. That shortcut ended up taking much longer than our regular route.

When we finally arrived back on base, the desk sergeant let us sign in quickly, but informed us that the night sergeant was about to check our quarters. We crept into the large barracks while the night inspection was in progress. Luckily, our beds were yet to be checked, so we quietly and quickly jumped into our beds, fully dressed with shoes still on. A close call, but we went undetected. Later on, Boudina and I would burst into laughter whenever we brought up the incident.

Journalists often visited the camp during training. They were always interested in snapping pictures of the five Dutch women soldiers smartly dressed in uniforms. Since I was clearly the youngest, not yet eighteen, I attracted considerable attention as the baby of the group.

My sense of humor vanished when I was called into a highly confidential meeting with several American lieutenants. They notified me that I had received excellent marks on my exams. While I was flattered by their praise, I didn't think that was the purpose of the meeting. They then informed me that I couldn't repeat anything they said. They were taking a group of WACs to France to help in the liberation of the country. Since none of the Americans spoke French, they wanted me to come along and act as an interpreter. They would take care of all the necessary paperwork, but, if I agreed to go, I couldn't tell anyone, not even my family. They said I could have a day to think about the decision, but impressed upon me that I was needed for the war effort.

I immediately fell into a quandary. The Americans had treated me wonderfully, and I really wanted to help. I was prepared to leave the Dutch WACs and do my duty, but I cringed at the thought of returning to France, a place filled with traumatic memories of death, escape, and survival that occurred just a few years ago. I had to tell them no. I felt guilty when I gave them my answer, wondering if I let them down, but I knew in my heart that I could not endure the thought of returning to France.

Had I accepted their offer, my life would have changed considerably. I would not have continued on to Australia and Indonesia with the Dutch Army, and I might never have met my future husband. I had already learned that life was unpredictable. Having made up my mind, I was prepared to move forward with my decision, not knowing where it would take me.

I soon received orders, along with the four other Dutch girls, to depart for California where we would await final instructions to depart for Australia. I looked forward to joining my two sisters who were already stationed there.

The five of us traveled to Riverside, California by train. We eventually arrived at a military hospital in Camp Haan where an entire wing had been prepared for us. Eight more Dutch girls expanded our contingent to thirteen WACs. Everyone was assigned a private room under the strict supervision of Lieutenant Dencher, a strict, middle-aged woman.

Since I had spent each of my previous six birthdays in a different city, it seemed appropriate that my eighteenth birthday would be celebrated in yet another location. I fondly remember that special event at Camp Haan. The Dutch women appeared at my door early in the morning, bearing presents and singing *Happy Birthday*. What a surprise! I was overwhelmed with emotion at the display of affection. When the women brought me into the dining room, the men stood up, placed me on the table, and sang *Happy Birthday* to me as well. That day became one of the most special moments in my life. Never did I expect that the army would offer such precious gifts of kindness and friendship.

While in Riverside, I was able to take advantage of some sightseeing. Someone provided all the Dutch women soldiers with passes and transportation to Metro-Goldwyn-Mayer movie studio. While at MGM, I met Jimmy Durante on his way into a studio. He stopped to chat with the lovely Dutch soldiers in beautiful blue uniforms and happily gave his autograph.

After two weeks, our platoon finally received our orders to go to Australia, where we would eventually depart for Indonesia after the country was freed from the Japanese. Our first stop was

San Francisco. While waiting for our ship, the army put us up in a boarding house and provided spending money. Lieutenant Dencher gave us permission to roam free for a few days. We truly deserved it, after three months of intense training. While free from military duties, we still had to wear our uniforms, something I didn't mind.

During my worldwide travels, I experienced many different types of food—Dutch, Belgian, French, Spanish, West Indian, and Cuban. It was now time to indulge in American cuisine. For breakfast, I would visit a small coffee shop that served wonderful pancakes, not crepes like I ate in Europe. I would order a pile of pancakes, smother them with syrup, and say, "*Dat is lekker!* That is good!"

Boudina had previously introduced me to popcorn in the movie theater. When she had mentioned that it was corn, I refused to eat it, telling her, "Where I come from, corn is pig feed." Upon her urging, I tasted the buttery, salty treat. From then on, I purchased my own super-sized bag of popcorn.

Boudina knew all the right things to eat. She introduced me to an ice cream shop where I ordered a huge chocolate milkshake, another thing I had never tasted. I loved my milkshakes, popcorn, pancakes, and French toast.

Our ship finally arrived in port. A Dutch freighter would carry us across the Pacific Ocean, some 7,800 miles. The crew enthusiastically welcomed the Dutch women soldiers, even though the sailors had to vacate their cabins. Back then, women were not allowed on a ship unless there was a doctor aboard. The freighter had a pharmacist as a member of the crew, but no doctor. Since the captain was eager to have us on his ship, he waived the rules. The women were a wonderful sight for sailors' eyes.

The cramped cabins contained bunk beds. Since I was the smallest and youngest, I was assigned a lower bunk with little room. I felt squashed, unable to sit up in bed. I had learned to put up with many inconveniences, so this seemed small compared to what I had been through.

Similar to my other travels on a ship during wartime, there were blackouts. Lights had to be extinguished at night. This concerned Lieutenant Dencher, because she couldn't see what was going on in the dark, especially with all the men aboard.

Originally, she didn't want us associating with the sailors, but with the long trans-Pacific journey ahead, she eventually allowed the Dutch women to interact with the staff. However, if a woman was invited to an officer's cabin, she could not enter alone. There had to be at least two women present, and the cabin doors had to remain open. Most of us would have liked fewer restrictions.

To ensure that the women were fully informed and protected, the lieutenant decided to conduct a sex education class. Many of the women didn't appreciate the lesson, since they were well educated in that area. Someone must've told the crew about our little seminar, because many of them crept outside the room and crouched at the door to listen.

The lieutenant began her talk, "Well, you know, a kiss on the mouth could…"

Before I could stop myself, I yelled out, *"Een kus op de mond, is voor het hart gezond,"* which rhymed in Dutch. Translated, it meant, "A kiss on the mouth is healthy for the heart."

My comment brought smiles from my friends, but a severe frown from the lieutenant. She immediately ordered me to her cabin. Feeling like a disobedient student, I opened the door and found officers quickly scurrying away. They weren't about to risk the wrath of Lieutenant Dencher.

Needless to say, I missed the rest of sex education. The irony of this whole episode was that, as the youngest woman, I was the one most in need of the lesson. While she was clearly trying to protect me, I feared that I would be forced to room with her for the rest of the trip.

As it so happened, a Dutch preacher and his wife were on board. I knew they liked me, because, as soon as they heard of the incident, they came down to the cabin.

The preacher told me, "Don't worry. We'll get you out of here."

They chuckled at my joke and intervened on my behalf. They eventually convinced the lieutenant to let me return to my own cabin. I much preferred the lower bunk than sleeping in a room with a strict lieutenant.

When we crossed the International Date Line, the crew threw a wonderful party. One of the sailors dressed up as Father Neptune. As the youngest member on board, I was made to sit on his lap. He razzed me about my age and told me I should have a baby bottle and pacifier. I laughed along with the crew, knowing it was all in good fun.

The rest of the voyage slipped right by until we arrived in Melbourne. I stood at attention with the rest of the Women's Army Corps as we pulled into the harbor. Excited about meeting Willy, whom I had not seen since Cuba, I anticipated a heartwarming reunion with my sister.

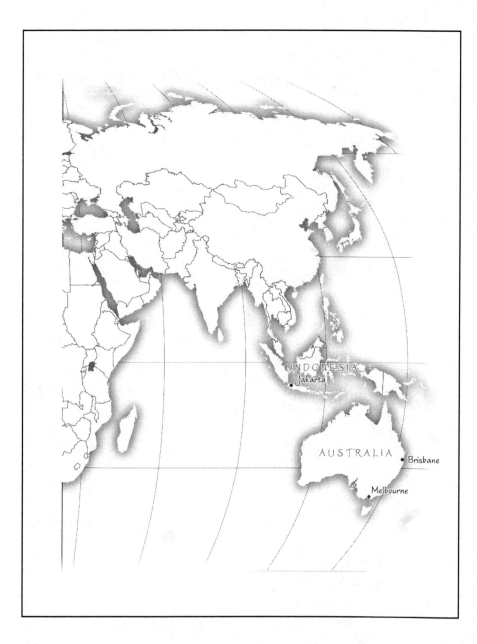

Military travels in Australia and Indonesia.

Chapter Ten

SISTERLY REUNION

Appreciate every person and enjoy life.

I proudly walked off the ship in August of 1945, wearing my Dutch uniform. My final destination was Brisbane, so I looked forward to the brief time with my sister in Melbourne. She worked in a military office there and arranged to have the day off to greet her little sister. Feeling overjoyed, I ran to Willy and hugged her tightly. We had been through so much together. Now we were admiring each other's smart uniforms marked with the Dutch Lion.

After I introduced Willy to the rest of the platoon, she joined us on the trip to the camp where we would stay one night. Willy was allowed to bunk temporarily with me in the barracks so we could catch up with one another. We had so much to share and so little time. We took advantage of each precious moment.

As it so happened, Dutch soldiers who were stationed in the same camp had organized a dance. Of course, my platoon wanted to join the party. The major in charge told us that the women could not socialize with the men, but could organize a dance among ourselves. We protested and wouldn't take no for an answer. We wanted to be with the boys. Lieutenant Dencher eventually stepped in and persuaded the major to allow us to attend. We jumped with joy at the news.

The Dutch boys had lined up a band and welcomed the women with open arms. Oh, how I enjoyed myself. Not only did I have my sister with me, but I celebrated my arrival in Australia with handsome Dutch soldiers. I partied until the lieutenant marshaled the troops to bed. After lights out, I chatted softly with Willy, who occupied the bed next to me. It was as if we had never been apart. I drifted off to sleep most grateful for the wonderful day.

Shortly after breakfast, I said farewell to Willy, knowing we would stay in touch and meet up again. My group then traveled north by train to Camp Columbia, a U.S. Army military camp in Wacol, near Brisbane, Queensland. Another reunion occurred, this time with Mary, who was stationed in the same camp. She made arrangements for us to share a room together. That turned out to last several months.

In the past, I had never felt all that comfortable with Mary. As the rebel in the family, she would sometimes take her anger out on me, since I was the youngest in the family. As a result, I learned to be cautious around her, unsure how she would react. Now that I was in the army, however, our relationship shifted. She treated me with greater respect.

On one of our weekends off, she took me to Brisbane for some sightseeing. We ended up at the zoo, one of the few places open on Sunday. I saw kangaroos and koala bears for the very first time. Of course, I had to hold one of the cuddly koalas, but I didn't stop there. At the snake exhibit, I paid a fee to have a python placed around my neck. Compared to what I had been through in life, a long snake slithering across my shoulders didn't seem all that scary. Mary captured that moment with her camera. I proudly placed that photograph among the growing collection of pictures depicting me in exotic locations.

Brisbane Zoo, Australia, 1945.

Brisbane Zoo, Yvonne, Mary, and cuddly friends.

Speaking of exotic, little did I realize that I would find myself in an intriguing job, deciphering secrets. I began working in the army code room at Camp Columbia, but shortly after starting the job, there came an opening in NEFIS, the Netherlands Forces Intelligence Service. When my new boss was called out on an emergency, I was left in charge. At eighteen, I ran a military intelligence service all by myself. Two Australian women, older than I was, handled the teletype. I managed the code. I must have done fairly well, because I remained there through March 1946, deciphering military telegrams that were received via teletype in code and transmitting secret outgoing messages. I could not have wished for a better job. I thoroughly enjoyed the detailed work as I played my part in military operations. I eventually received a letter of commendation. (See Appendix A.)

Strangely, my ability to maintain silence and hold secrets became an integral part of my responsibilities. Since NEFIS was top secret, I was sworn to a code of silence. I couldn't talk with anyone about my activities, not even with my sisters. The messages and telegrams for coding or deciphering came from

High Command and dealt with a range of war activities, such as the locations of ships, movement of troops, and enemy positions. These secrets I happily kept.

In an odd twist of fate, Mary and I became involved with refugees. We started helping Dutch women and children who were liberated from Indonesian concentration camps and brought over by ship to our military camp. Only a few years ago, we were like them, refugees without a home. I knew only too well what they must have gone through, confined in unsanitary conditions, unsure about their fate. To boost the morale, the military women wrote and produced a play with skits that were performed one evening. I created and sewed nearly all of the costumes for the performances. I never grew tired of handicrafts, nor of helping refugees.

With the war over in Europe, the conflict still raged with Japan. The Dutch East Indies, now Indonesia, was finally liberated from the Japanese who had occupied the islands in 1942. The first wave of Dutch troops moved in during September 1945. Months later, Willy received her orders to serve in Jakarta. Before she left Australia, my sister flew to Brisbane for a few nights. The three sisters were once again reunited, albeit for a short period. We made the most of our time together. A few months after Willy departed, my orders arrived at the same time as Mary's. Both of us would be off on another adventure.

An important lesson in families is to treat one another with respect.

Jakarta, Indonesia, 1946.

NEFIS Headquarters.

Chapter Eleven

INDONESIA

No matter what nationality, race or color, there really is no difference.

Indonesia had been a Dutch colony when it was invaded by the Japanese, who then forced their Dutch prisoners into concentration camps. With liberation came rebuilding and lots of hard work. Our unit flew by military plane, which meant minimal comfort. Two long rows of seats packed with soldiers without seatbelts made for a bumpy ride. The army never promised first-class travel. Our transport arrived in Soerabaja, now Surabaya, the second largest city in Indonesia.

When we stayed overnight with the crew, I had the chance to attend an open-air movie theater where everyone sat in lounge chairs. Indonesia's climate was hot and humid, so watching a picture in the outdoors provided immediate relief. The movie itself wasn't memorable, but I found the experience of gazing at a large silver screen under the stars entertaining.

The next day our group continued to Batavia, now Jakarta, the largest city and capital of Indonesia. Mary and I met up with Willy, who was already working in a military office. Our family reunion was brief, since Mary was sent to work in Bandung, the capital of West Java province in Indonesia.

Jakarta airport, 1946.

Yvonne and Willy, third and fourth from left.

I was fortunate to share a large room in a convent with Willy and three other military women. The nuns occupied the back of the building, while we lived in the front. To offset the hot, sticky climate, we kept the windows open. However, that meant plenty of mosquitoes. We covered our beds with netting as a defense against the nasty insects.

The convent became my new home. I so enjoyed the tasty Dutch and Indonesian food that the nuns cooked for us. My favorite dish was *Rijsttafel,* an Indonesian rice specialty with small side dishes of fish, satay, and vegetables. I would smack my lips and say, "*Dat is lekker!* That is good!"

Since we all became very busy, one of the women at the convent hired a maid who charged each of us twenty-five cents a week. I was more than happy to let someone else clean and iron my clothes. The first and last time I used an iron heated with coals, I burned a shirt. I needed those shirts *without* brown marks. I gladly let the maid wash and press my uniforms, even my personal clothes. Clean sheets were provided by the nuns, and if the maid arrived early enough, she'd make our beds. Not having any housework freed me to fulfill my new responsibilities.

I was sent to the head office of the Netherlands Forces Intelligence Service, conveniently housed next door to the convent. I worked with two sergeants and my boss, who was most likely a captain at the time. The four of us got along extremely well as we deciphered military telegrams that arrived in secret code and transferred any outgoing messages into code. Since the office stayed open after hours, someone had to remain on duty to handle urgent messages.

Shortly after I arrived in Jakarta, I became a sergeant, not that it made much of a difference to me. My workday began at 8:00 a.m., but since one staff member had to stay after 5:00 p.m. until the work was done, that often meant I wouldn't arrive back at the convent until after midnight. There were many long days. On Fridays and Saturdays, the convent stayed open until 1:00 a.m., so the military women could stay out late. The extra hours meant that my late night was often spent at the office. I placed great importance on my duties and, therefore, took little time to socialize. No one was allowed in our office except the military police, who brought telegrams for us to decipher or picked up the ones we finished. Because of the dangerous conditions, women were not allowed alone on the streets after 7:00 p.m. I was required to call an MP to escort me home after hours, even though I lived across the street.

Military women received special protection against insurgents. This was also extended to the nuns in the convent. The extra security precautions were necessary, since the Governor-General's palace stood right across the street. The Governor-General, Hubertus van Mook, functioned as the president of the colonial government, so everyone called him president.

Early one morning, I awoke to the sound of gunfire. I rushed to the second-floor window where our bedroom overlooked the palace. Horrified, I watched the Governor-General's secretary getting kidnapped. Terrorists pulled him out of his car at the side of the building and murdered some of the guards. I witnessed the kidnappers' car speeding away with the secretary as prisoner. He was never seen again.

On another frightening night, a military woman from the convent was kidnapped while hitchhiking, not the smartest move on her part. She escaped certain death because, as a native Indonesian, she happened to be familiar with the route the kidnappers took. At one point, she jumped out of the Jeep and rushed down one of the canals that ran through the city. She crept along the canal until she was discovered by the military police. Everyone in the convent stayed up late, worrying sick that she would be killed. We breathed a collective sigh of relief when she was found and taken to the hospital without major injuries.

Because of the military protection at night, the MPs were allowed to walk into the convent and inspect our rooms if they suspected something was wrong. They sometimes took advantage of the situation. I once saw a couple of soldiers walk into our room with flashlights, checking out the girls rather than hunting for intruders.

Every evening, one of the women was assigned to cover the reception desk of the convent to let others know when a male visitor arrived. I was spared that duty because I was on call twenty-four hours, in case something pressing had to be deciphered.

Since most of the women had been going out with their boyfriends, the officer in charge wanted one night for the women to socialize together. She implemented a policy stating that on Thursday evenings, the women were not allowed to leave the convent at night. I, of course, was excluded from that rule because of my work, which had a few advantages.

Willy was angry about the confinement because her boyfriend, an English officer, was leaving the following Thursday evening to return to England. Willy decided to spend the evening with him anyway and told me to keep quiet about the matter. No problem for me. I had plenty of experience with the secret business. Unfortunately, my sister was caught and punished by having to stay in for two weeks. She didn't care, since she had the chance to spend precious time with her boyfriend before he left.

Though I frequently worked over the weekend, I didn't mind. I loved my work and felt like I was making a real contribution. Any messages that needed to be coded or deciphered were brought in by the military police. Using a secret system, I either created code or deciphered military messages that dealt with a broad range of war activities. After typing up the code or intended meaning, I would place it in an envelope that I sealed with a rubber stamp. I would then call the military police to deliver the envelope to the assigned official.

The long hours at the office were immensely rewarding; however, they did affect my relationship with Willy, who worked an eight-to-five shift. She often complained about not seeing me. She knew I worked for NEFIS and avoided asking questions. Of course, I was sworn to secrecy, so I didn't dare volunteer any information. Silence and secrecy had become integral parts of my life.

Throughout my working day, I remained in the steaming, hot office housed in a two-story building. Without any air conditioning in Jakarta, the second-floor office felt like a furnace. To create ventilation, doors were usually left open. Guards with rifles stood outside the building to ensure that only authorized persons entered.

On one particular Sunday, I was working alone in the office and heard someone enter the room. At first, I thought it was the military police delivering confidential telegrams. Instead of a soldier, a huge monkey reared its head. Somehow, it sneaked past the guards through the open door. So much for security!

When the monkey and I saw each other, we both jumped in fright. It screeched and hopped onto the desk. Some of the monkeys in Jakarta could be vicious if they attacked, so I quickly searched for an exit. My eyes scanned for the key to the adjoining locked office where I could call a guard on the phone. Somehow, the clever monkey followed my eyes and, before I could grab it, snatched the key.

Holding its prize, the monkey ran around the office screaming and throwing my papers in the air. I stood there horrified, not only at the screeching, but because my stack of confidential papers had been scattered over the floor. Thankfully, the monkey decided it was through playing mischief and scampered down the stairs, leaving the place in a mess.

I rushed downstairs to shut the door, cursing the creature and the guards who were supposed to prevent unauthorized visitors. I returned to the office and picked up the papers, then called my boss and told him about the harrowing experience. I needed a rest from the commotion and went home without finishing my work, something I rarely did. The next day, I was mercilessly teased by the men in my office. They chuckled as they told me that it could only happen to me, the one girl in the office.

Mind you, most of the time, I enjoyed being the only woman. The men treated me like an equal, as each person had a specialized job. On my nineteenth birthday, the two sergeants and the captain decorated the floor around my desk with potted plants. I was touched by their thoughtfulness. That event marked the eighth year in a row that I celebrated my birthday in a different city. I hoped that my next birthday would be held in Belgium with my parents and sisters.

Although I was in Jakarta, I was surrounded by many Dutch people. Across the street at the Governor-General's Palace, Hubertus van Mook often held cocktail parties. The president always invited the Dutch women soldiers. Initially, I was impressed when I entered the palace and shook hands with him and the other important dignitaries. There was plenty to drink and eat, and I had fun mixing in the crowd. On the second occasion, I couldn't be bothered with all the pomp. And as far as the food, the nuns in the convent cooked wonderful Indonesian meals that I preferred. While the president continued to hold his cocktail parties, I never felt inclined to return.

Occasionally, I would take a day off. I once joined a group of male and female soldiers who visited one of the local islands. We found more monkeys. Some of the men played a trick on them by placing food on the ground beneath the monkeys' tree. Everyone pretended to sleep while the monkeys slowly climbed down from their branches and made their way for the treats. As soon as they reached for a snack, everyone would sit up tall and make a scene. The monkeys scattered. Angry about missing out on a meal, they screamed with revenge, throwing whatever they could grab. We scampered out of missile range. Never mess with a monkey!

My dear friend Boudina happened to be stationed in Jakarta. Unfortunately, I rarely saw her because our work schedules kept us so busy. She fell in love, and as often happened during wartime in foreign cities, she married her boyfriend, an English officer. I joyously attended Boudina's wedding and celebrated the day with her and friends.

I continued working with NEFIS in Indonesia until October, 1946. My parents had since moved back to Belgium, seeking to restart their lives. Willy, Mary, and I were anxious to join them, so decided to end our tour in the army and return home. When my sisters and I signed up for military service, we agreed to remain until six months after the liberation of Indonesia. With the Japanese surrendering in September of 1945 and the Dutch troops arriving in Jakarta at the end of that month, we had stayed well past our initial commitment. We placed a formal request to leave the army.

One afternoon, I received a call that I had to depart the next morning by ship to Surabaya. The ocean liner *DSM Klipfontein*, brought into service for the war, was set to sail to Surabaya and pick up women and children recently freed from the Indonesian concentration camps. It would then return to Jakarta to collect my sisters, Dutch nurses, and other personnel wanting to return to the Netherlands. The ocean liner required that a woman be on board to help with the refugees. I was the chosen one.

D.S.M. „KLIPFONTEIN"

DSM Klipfontein

As it turned out, I didn't get a chance to say goodbye to my friends, but in the army, I learned to follow orders. Packing a duffle bag was simple: merely toss in my belongings and throw the strap over my shoulder. Not surprisingly, I was the youngest military person on board, and a woman, to boot, so the captain had the first officer move out of his cabin to make room for me. The captain wasn't pleased that I was on board because of the added responsibility of looking after a woman on his ship. To protect me from the advances of his sailors, he kept a close eye on me, which wasn't difficult since my cabin happened to be next to his. I was ordered not to open the windows, and to lock the door at all times. Additionally, I had to eat my meals at the table with the doctor and dentist. They were both young, so I didn't mind their company in the least.

In Surabaya, we picked up a couple hundred Dutch refugees who were mothers and children. I had plenty to do, as they were in poor health. My job was to register each refugee before they could board. They were then ushered to the lower level of the ship where they spent their time. They slept on cots, with the deafening noise that occurred in the lower level, but then again, the concentration camps were far worse than a noisy, cramped ship. Fortunately, some of the sailors helped make the refugees comfortable.

An army officer, presumably a captain, was assigned to work with the refugees. He knew of my past work with NEFIS and was impressed with my credentials. He asked me to assist him during the trip to the Netherlands. Since I was still under oath as a sergeant, I started working the minute we left Jakarta.

Before leaving the city where I had lived for almost seven months, I spent a couple of days saying goodbye to my friends in the military. I felt a mixture of emotions—sad about leaving the army, which had become a second family, yet excited about seeing my parents again and returning to private life.

When it was time to leave Indonesia on October 19, 1946, my sisters and I boarded the ocean liner, along with the nurses and other Dutch people returning home. The sailors moved out of their quarters to make room for all the women. I shared a cabin with my sisters and a bunch of nurses. Another tight squeeze for everyone.

Though the hours were long, I enjoyed my work with the refugees during the voyage. It seemed strange that I was again helping others who were displaced from their homes. The captain taught me how to interview the refugee mothers so we would have an accurate record of any injustices. I typed reports late into the night with the captain so the paperwork would be completed before reaching the Netherlands. He and I worked well together and actually finished processing all the papers before dropping anchor in Rotterdam.

I typed my final report in the Dutch Indonesian Army as Sergeant Yvonne de Leeuwe and prepared for a new life with my sisters and parents. I wasn't sure what I would find in Europe, but I hoped all would work out for the best.

Arriving in Rotterdam, November, 1946.

Three sisters in uniform, left to right–Yvonne, Willy, and Mary.

Chapter Twelve

RETURNING HOME

Home – you never realize how much you miss it.

I had been corresponding regularly with my parents when I left Cuba, so I knew they had started a new life in Belgium. They were anxious to be reunited as a family. After sailing over 7,000 miles, the ship finally docked in Rotterdam, the Netherlands on November 20, 1946. I found my parents waiting expectantly for us. My sisters and I, still wearing our uniforms, rushed to greet my mother and father. We hugged and cried, so happy to be together once again. We had survived the war.

We spent considerable time sharing our stories of survival and adventure with one another. My parents were living in Antwerp, a major city that dealt with diamonds. Not surprisingly, my father had a job cutting the precious jewels. He told us that Belgium was the better place to live after the war than the Netherlands, which was facing severe food and housing shortages.

On the drive to Amsterdam, I witnessed the impact of the war. Houses had been destroyed, piles of rubble littered the city, and refugees streamed back into town, causing massive overcrowding. Signs of reconstruction appeared everywhere. Since there weren't enough available homes, families were forced to take in homeless individuals. This was enforced by the government to maximize accommodations.

Our first stop was to visit my younger cousin, Mary van Loon, who was three years old the last time I saw her. She had been through her own story of survival, having been sent by her parents—my mother's youngest brother, Louis, and his wife, Roos—to live with a Dutch farmer. Shortly after her brother Abby was born, he also went to another farming couple. They raised him as their own son, as a Catholic. Mary and Abby's parents, like many Dutch Jews, tragically lost their lives in a concentration camp. Their daring action to save their children enabled Mary and Abby to survive the war.

At ten years of age, Mary now lived with relatives from her mother's side. Abby was still living with his foster parents and would rejoin her at a later date. I loved seeing Mary again, yet I couldn't help but feel the tremendous loss as I heard about all the family members who had died in the concentration camps. The Van Loon side of the family lost two aunts and five uncles, plus their spouses and their children. Our once large, extended family had been decimated by the Nazis, with only two uncles and two cousins surviving from my mother's side. I thought about my brother and wondered if he suffered a horrible fate.

My father didn't have news of his own side of the family, the De Leeuwes, and feared the worst. However, he never lost hope that Marcel, his only son, was still alive. He had contacted the Red Cross, but they couldn't shed any light on his disappearance. He thought Marcel might have ended up in an internment camp in Russia. Or possibly started a new life in Europe, believing we had died in the war. My father bore tremendous guilt about signing the paper from the woman with the underground. If she were a German spy, she would have handed Marcel over to the Nazis. That was too unbearable a thought, so my father kept on believing Marcel was alive, somewhere.

Not knowing what happened to my brother added to the pain that I kept hidden. If he was still living, he would have carried his tools in his pocket, anxious to help others fix their machines. Whenever I saw a young man who resembled Marcel, I wanted to shout to him and see if he was my brother. Marcel's absence left a gaping hole in my life.

Bearing the grief, I traveled with my family to Antwerp. We lived with my mother's brother and his wife, Joseph and Susan van Loon, for a short time. Joseph and my mother lost their seven other siblings in the death camps.

I was not alone in my grief. The Dutch Jews who survived had lost countless family members in the concentration camps. So many innocent lives had been terminated. One way I coped with the suffering was to avoid dwelling on it. Just as the broken and torn homes had to be rebuilt, I had to create a new life with the remaining members of my family. I was fortunate to have survived. I couldn't squander the opportunity to make something of my life.

My sisters and I went to the Dutch Consulate to obtain our final discharge papers from the army. On November 29, 1946, the three of us were no longer sergeants in the Dutch Indonesian Army. We officially became private citizens.

As my eighteenth birthday had occurred overseas, I had to choose whether to be a Belgian or Dutch citizen. I had just left the army, so decided to keep my Dutch citizenship, even though I felt more Belgian, having been born in Antwerp.

When I was stationed in Indonesia, I never received any payment for military service. I had been told that money would be kept in a savings account and could be accessed once I returned to the Netherlands. When I asked about the back pay, I was informed that since Indonesia had claimed independence, they were responsible for the payment. Their answer meant that I had served seven months in Indonesia for free. I tried repeatedly to correct the problem, writing to officials, but got nowhere. The shocking reality sank in: I had returned home without any money.

Fortunately, with all the reconstruction, it was fairly easy for me and my sisters to obtain work. Willy and Mary found jobs in an office, and I began working in Brussels for the AJDC, the American Joint Distribution Committee. I was involved in the importing of food from the United States, which then had to be exported to different countries for the people who survived the concentration camps. In my own small way, I was able to help the survivors.

I knew my officer manager job was temporary, but it paid well. Once the new building in Antwerp was completed to replace the old one that had been bombed, my boss Mr. Cohen and I moved the shipping department there. Two young men were hired to work for me.

I was nineteen at the time when I began working for Mr. Cohen. He and his wife had lost family during the war and didn't have any children. They became very fond of me and affectionately treated me as if I was their daughter. At fifty-eight, Mr. Cohen was seven years older than my father. He was so enamored with me and my work that he wanted to adopt me. When I translated his request in French for my father who spoke only Dutch, I replied before my father could answer. "I already have parents."

Mr. Cohen accepted the decision gracefully but continued to treat me as if I was part of his family. He paid me three to four bonuses per year out of his own pocket. Those funds, added to the excellent salary from the AJDC, allowed me to build my new life and grow a solid bank account.

Meanwhile, my father found a large, two-bedroom apartment for the five of us, with my sisters and I sharing one bedroom. My mother stayed at home in the traditional role of housewife — cooking, cleaning, and washing clothes. Everyone fell into a routine of work, family life, and socializing.

I started attending the Maccabi Club, a Jewish organization for young people. They sponsored dances, chess games, Ping-Pong, bridge, and other social activities. I made wonderful friends and eventually found love.

*One way to cope with suffering is to
avoid dwelling on the pain.*

Antwerp, Belgium, 1948.

George Cardozo marries Yvonne de Leeuwe.

Chapter Thirteen

FINDING LOVE

When you find real love, you feel normal again.

I wasn't looking for love when a fellow took me to the Maccabi Club to play Ping-Pong. As it so happened, a series of chess matches was underway. I had learned chess in one of the refugee homes in France, so became intrigued with the ongoing games. I met the organizer, George Cardozo, a five-foot-ten, shy, twenty-year-old man with dark-rimmed glasses. Ten months younger, I was immediately struck by his light blue eyes and curly reddish-blond hair. When he and I chatted, I discovered a number of similarities, including the fact that I had once lived in the same building as his aunt and uncle. He clearly wanted to spend more time talking, but couldn't that night because he was responsible for organizing the chess games.

I found out later that he knew we were meant to be together. So much so that he devised a plan to steer me away from the fellow who took me to the club. He phoned his friend, Willy Zomerplaag, and told him to come over to the club and take me home. However, George instructed Willy that he couldn't get involved because George's eyes were set on me. Willy came and chatted with me for some time, and before I knew it, he walked me home instead of the boy who brought me to the club.

I had been dating others, but George seemed to be the one. I felt special whenever we spent time together. We often went to the Maccabi Club, where we learned to play bridge. He enjoyed games, just like me. After several months, we broke up briefly over a misunderstanding, but resumed our courtship when I contracted scarlet fever. I couldn't work for six weeks and stayed at home, feeling miserable. George found out about my illness and brought over a box of chocolates. He wanted to get back together. How could I refuse such a sweet offer from a real gentleman?

George at nineteen.

As I recovered, we started courting more seriously. George didn't have much money at the time, so we made do with limited resources. We walked in the park, swam in the public pool, attended movies, and visited the local shops to admire their wares.

We had many things in common. Not only were we the same age, but we were born in Antwerp to Dutch parents. We were both shy, George painfully so, and missed out on a lot of schooling because of the war. He was an only child and escaped Belgium with his parents on the same day my family left. He stayed in a Dutch refugee house in Toulouse around the same time that my family lived in another refugee home in Lessac. George eventually joined the Maquis, the French resistance fighters. While he never talked about his time in the resistance, I suspected there were dreadful memories he wanted to forget. His father was forced into labor and disappeared like my brother, never to be seen again.

George maintained silence and secrets about the war, just like me. He was as closed about the past as I was. We both avoided talking about the memories of war, hoping to put them behind us.

He had been close to his father, so losing him to the war and not knowing what happened to him left its mark. I had felt similar pain over the loss of my brother. We both carried our grief but never burdened each other with the details.

On hindsight, I would have wanted to break the silence and talk openly about the past with George. It would have helped both of us let go of the secrets, so we could've healed from the wounds of war. If I had opened up, George may have followed my lead. Unfortunately, that never happened. Still, the two of us would forge a deep bond that would last forever.

When the war was over, George had returned to Belgium with his mother. He began to learn the diamond business, but didn't much care for it. He eventually got involved with selling insurance. When I met him, he wasn't earning any money, but he was exceptionally bright and had grand plans.

George and I had been dating about six months when he proposed, affectionately calling me, "*Schat*, sweetheart."

Being in love, I heartily accepted. However, I was afraid my father would object. He wanted his older girls to marry first. Ever so shy, George quietly approached my father to ask for my hand in marriage. Alone with my father, he was so nervous that my father quickly said yes before George could complete his request. My father felt that he had lost his boy in the war, but with George, he regained a son. Dad loved George like a son and treated him extremely well.

After we were officially engaged in May of 1948, we purchased a lottery ticket. Miraculously, we won. Back then, the amount wasn't huge, but was enough to purchase fabric for velvet drapes for our new place. Using my mother's old-fashioned Singer machine with a foot pedal, I proudly sewed beautiful drapes, my first large creation that would hang in our home. I was excited about a new life with George.

Unfortunately, my boss Mr. Cohen wasn't pleased with my choice. He was seven years older than my dad and always insisted that he should pick the man for me to marry. Shortly after getting engaged, I walked into the office to find Mr. Cohen waiting with Mr. Kaplan. Acting as a matchmaker, my boss wanted me to take Mr. Kaplan around Antwerp and show him the sights. I was afraid to tell Mr. Cohen the truth, but felt compelled to let him know of my upcoming marriage.

Upon hearing the news, Mr. Cohen became quite angry. He was probably embarrassed, as well, because Mr. Kaplan traveled all the way from Germany to meet me. My boss always told me to wait for the right one to come along.

I had done just that when I found George.

To verify that I had chosen an upstanding man, my boss insisted on meeting my fiancé. George, ever so shy, visited Mr. Cohen in his office. After the meeting, my boss took me aside. He told me that he was unhappy with my choice and that I deserved a better husband than one who sold insurance.

In some ways, Mr. Cohen treated me like an overprotective father who wanted the best for me. George and I decided to use his rabbi for the service, hoping that would convey the message that we appreciated all that he had done, and that he would give his blessing. Unfortunately, he did not. I was saddened by his response. He did, however, attend the traditional Jewish wedding, and acted as best man to please me.

George and I organized a grand wedding. My parents paid for the banquet hall and trimmings, and I added some money of my own to celebrate in style. Following the European tradition to have two ceremonies, one civil and the other religious, George and I were married on September 9, 1948. Mr. Cohen's rabbi spoke only French, so George met him prior to the ceremony to teach him the marital vows in Dutch. Feeling quite nervous, I stood, in my white wedding gown and veil, next to George, in his dark blue suit and hat. I followed the rabbi's instructions and happily repeated the vow, "*Ik neem je als mijn man.* I take you as my husband."

George gladly repeated, "*Ik neem je als mijn vrouw.* I take you as my wife."

We both sipped wine from a small glass, then George placed it on the floor and crushed it with his foot. The guests shouted, "*Mazel Tov,*" wishing us good luck as husband and wife.

We enjoyed a lovely reception and formal dinner with friends and family. Afterward, George and I spent a night in Antwerp, then took a train to spend two wonderful weeks on vacation in the Netherlands, where we stayed in lovely hotels. We were both bashful, but spent the two weeks really getting to know each other. He lovingly called me "Von," while I called him "Jos." We went out for meals and treated ourselves to one of our favorite activities — dancing. We made a dashing couple on the dance floor, particularly with the tango and Viennese waltz. One evening, we became so absorbed in the music and dancing that the other dancers left the floor to watch us perform. When I saw all the eyes staring, I became self-conscious and told George we should stop. He held me close and told me, "We were meant to dance together."

How could I resist him? The people watching broke into applause. That was a night to remember.

Upon our return, we took up residence in the two-bedroom apartment that George and his mother, Rachel, had occupied. Rachel left to live with friends so we could have our own place, which happened to be a mere twenty-minute walk from my parents. George spruced up our apartment with fresh paint and wallpaper. With the wedding gifts of furniture, dishes, and other household items to make our home comfortable, we started our life together.

My job with the American Joint Distribution Committee came to an end, but I maintained contact with Mr. and Mrs. Cohen for many years. George continued to sell insurance, and I found a job sorting diamonds, which paid quite well, even though I only worked two to three days a week, depending upon the arrival of the diamond shipment.

I must say that the first year of marriage was difficult. George and I had so much to learn about one another. We had different personalities and different ways to handle problems. When I would get upset, I would cry, and that would upset George. When he was troubled, he would withdraw, and that would upset me. However, we never went to bed without making up.

After a while, we learned to recognize our strengths and accept our differences. We were both hard workers and appreciated the simple things in life, having had the experience of losing everything during the war. We hired a cleaning woman to help care for the apartment, and, after two years of marriage, George bought our first car, an old, burgundy, 1929 convertible Mercedes Benz. The radiator leaked, the top couldn't come down, and the car often had to be pushed to get started. Actually, it had no business being on the road, but we did manage to coax some miles out of it.

George fixing 1929 Mercedes Benz.

Our neighbors detested our prized Mercedes when we left it parked in front of the building. One day, they threw vegetable scraps on top of our beloved car. George was so angry that he drove the Mercedes to the police to file a report against the neighbors. I couldn't help but laugh as I watched the car move down the street with potato peelings and garbage tumbling off the roof. That news event even found its way into the papers. I imagined the article reading, *"Trashed Mercedes."*

Soon thereafter, we got rid of the car. Public transportation was faster and more reliable than our old Mercedes. And we didn't have to worry about neighbors tossing garbage.

I wanted to start a family, but George wasn't as keen. He was afraid that another war would break out in Europe and didn't want his children to suffer what we had endured when we escaped the German occupation. However, I really wanted children, and was blessed when our first child, Paul, was born in 1951. As the proud parents of our son, George and I invited my sisters and our parents to the hospital to see the new baby. Everyone was so excited, especially the grandparents. I even extended an invitation to Mr. and Mrs. Cohen to visit our child. Only Mrs. Cohen came to the hospital. She apologized that her husband didn't want to see the baby. He still carried a grudge that I married George.

I stopped working and stayed home with Paul while George continued in the insurance business. My son looked just like his father, with curly, red hair. Later on, he reminded me of my brother, Marcel, when he made a funny face. Paul was an easy baby and brought me immense pleasure.

Before our marriage, George had requested that I not make soup. Apparently, his mother's recipe wasn't very tasty. Since I loved to cook, I told my father about my dilemma. He wisely advised me to cook meals my way and not worry about George. I followed my father's suggestion. After George tasted my delicious broths, he couldn't live without them. He loved my chicken soup made with fresh chickens and little meatballs and my Dutch lentil soup with flour dumplings. For a special dessert, I made *boterkoek*, Dutch butter cake.

Ever since we had married, George and I had talked about leaving Belgium. With Joseph Stalin running the Soviet Union, Russia grew as a world power. The Cold War escalated, as did the tension in Europe. We decided to leave Belgium rather than take the risk of staying and facing another invasion or Holocaust. Our choices were to immigrate to Australia or to the United States. If we moved to the U.S., George would have had to enlist in the armed service and leave me alone with Paul. We didn't want any more separations. Though we preferred to live in the U.S., where there seemed more opportunities, we chose Montreal, Canada, where George could use his perfect French. We hoped to immigrate later to the United States.

George and I sold all our possessions and bought a large trunk for most of our belongings. We wanted to leave before Paul was a year old because he could travel with us without a ticket on the transatlantic journey by ship.

My sisters and parents were also planning to leave Europe, but they wanted to resettle in South America. Since many of the diamonds came from Brazil, my father hoped to find immediate work there in the business he knew so well. Willy and Mary left for Brazil shortly after I immigrated to Canada, and were later followed by my parents. Our family was on the move again.

I was ready to start over again, this time with husband and child.

Beaconfield, Canada, 1956.

From left to right – George, Vivian, Yvonne, and Paul.

Chapter Fourteen

STARTING OVER

No matter how many times you start over, don't give up.

We left Rotterdam in 1952 on the *SS Rijndam*, three days before Paul's first birthday. The ship rocked and rolled so much, I spent the entire trip sick. My husband took care of Paul while I spent my time in the bathroom throwing up. I was so grateful when the ship finally pulled into the harbor.

The arrival in Halifax, Nova Scotia brought a small disaster. Carrying our suitcases, we waited for the large trunk to be lowered off the ship. I watched in horror as the large box fell from the crane and crashed onto the pavement. Our possessions were flattened. Now we had to start over in a country without our prized belongings. I remembered when I was twelve years old and escaped with my family to France. Back then, we traveled with just the clothes on our backs. Starting over with nothing seemed part of life.

George and I had moved and resettled countless times, so losing our belongings was a minor bump in the road. We were young and had each other, plus a young child. We joined the group of displaced persons from the ship who were starting a new life, like us, in Montreal. We all took a crowded train overnight from Halifax to the Canadian province of Quebec. We slept on uncomfortable wooden benches and eagerly looked forward to a soft bed.

We rented a room from a family who lived in the house. Our room was so tiny I couldn't walk around the bed. We couldn't handle the cramped conditions, especially with a one-year-old child. Though we had paid one month's rent, we left after two weeks. Fortunately, George quickly found a job selling insurance, we rented an apartment. Being able to speak French made the transition much easier, as most people in Montreal spoke the language. Like me, George had a strong work ethic. As he sold insurance, money flowed in and we saved for a house.

One year after moving to Canada, in 1953, I received the sad news that my father died of cancer in Brazil. I cried many tears. I felt so bad for my father, who was only fifty-seven years old. He never truly had a chance to live a full, happy life. The war had stolen many precious years. He never found out what happened to my brother, but always believed that Marcel survived the war. Another lesson I had learned was that death was a part of life. It didn't make grieving any easier; it just meant I had to accept it.

Fortunately, another precious life appeared with our second child, Vivian, who arrived in 1955. My family was now complete with a son and daughter. As my sisters and I had developed different personalities, so did my children. While Paul tended to be quiet and reflective, Vivian was more chatty and inquisitive.

We proudly purchased our first house outside Montreal. As often happened with first homes, there were flaws. While the large, four-bedroom house was very spacious and included a basement finished with knotty pine, the basement flooded when the snow melted. That first flood ruined some of the furniture. Again, I learned to take the bad with the good.

I settled into a routine of caring for the family, cooking my soups, sewing clothes, and caring for the house. I made all my outfits as well as the clothes for my children and husband. Using my hands and working with fabrics and designing clothes brought tremendous joy. I bought patterns and changed them to fit my own design. If it hadn't been for the war, I would have been a dress designer.

While I truly enjoyed raising my family, the one aspect of parenting that brought considerable worry was when Paul or Vivian became ill. Because of my experience during the war, I worried myself sick about losing them. Besides George, they became the most precious aspects of my life. While there weren't any major health concerns, I was always concerned about their welfare.

At one point, George's mother, Rachel, left Belgium and came to live with us. She found a job in a department store and offered my children the wonderful experience of having a grandmother at home. They adored Granny Ray.

My family lived in Canada for almost seven years—a happy and prosperous period. However, the extremes in weather became oppressive. During one winter day, the temperature dropped to forty below zero. That prompted me and George to make yet another move, this time to sunny California.

Since George's mother had established herself in Canada, she didn't want to relocate, so she remained in Montreal. Comings and goings had become a part of my life. Though I felt sad leaving her behind, I had to move forward with my young family.

With our immigration documents in order, we relocated to California, and within a year, we bought a three-bedroom house in Norwalk, a suburban city in Los Angeles County. During that time, my mother remarried, to a Dutchman and lived in Anaheim. George continued to sell insurance and provide for the family, while I cared for the children. They had the opportunity to receive a wonderful education, something George and I both missed out on because of the war. He had a brilliant, inquisitive mind and was always reading books from the library. If given the chance, he would have liked to have been a doctor, while I would have pursued fashion design. One of the casualties of war was lost opportunities. Fortunately, our children benefited from living in an abundant, free country.

After five years in California, George and I proudly became citizens of the United States. At that time, we wanted to Americanize our name to fit into our adopted country. After discussing many alternatives for Cardozo, we chose Carson and included that name on our citizenship papers. George and I proudly attended the induction ceremony with our two children. Paul wore his first suit, which I had sewn for the occasion, and Vivian beamed in her handmade dress. How proud we were. After all the years of moving from country to country, we found our home in the United States.

As the children spent their days at school, I felt a growing desire to work. George, having a European mindset, didn't want his wife working outside the house. He saw my role as the homemaker. However, I had been introduced to Avon and wanted to sell the products. George laughed at the prospect, telling me I was too shy to talk to a lot of people. I truly wanted to work, so I signed up to be a distributor and told him after the fact. I had to prove that I could be successful selling, just like him. After all, even though he had been a bashful boy, he learned to make a good living as an insurance salesman. As it turned out, I sold Avon for seven years and became quite successful. I brought in extra income, became more social, and in the process, made many friends.

We eventually moved to a larger home, this time in La Habra, a city in the northwestern corner of Orange County. For twelve years, we lived in the residential community that offered great schools for Paul and Vivian to continue their education.

Following the tradition established by my parents, I kept Friday evenings free for family activities. Sundays were also set aside for the children. George and I would drink coffee and read the newspaper before our son and daughter woke up. They would eventually join us in the living room where we would read and plan our day together. Whatever the children wanted for brunch, I would make, though crepes were their favorite. Since George and I had missed out on a childhood, we avoided discussions about war and encouraged Paul and Vivian to enjoy being children. We took many family outings to Knott's Berry Farm and, of course, Disneyland.

Music became part of the household. Paul played the trumpet and Vivian the violin and cello. George loved opera. Every Saturday, he would listen on the radio to the full-length operatic presentations from the Metropolitan Opera sponsored by Texaco. He would listen to the music for hours.

On Wednesdays, George would stay home, so the two of us could catch up on the bookkeeping for his insurance clients. Before we purchased an adding machine, I would write the numbers in the ledger, then add up the final figures. Once we completed our work, we would treat ourselves to a lovely meal at a nice restaurant.

When not helping George, I returned to my sewing. I used the Ping-Pong table in the garage to lay out my fabrics, and set up the electric sewing machine, which sure made my job easier. No phone books on a manual foot pedal, like I had done as a child. I made shirts and pants for George and Paul and dresses for Vivian. She was thrilled with the special outfits that I made for her Barbie, who wore miniature outfits in the same style and fabric as the clothes I created. Her doll became the best-dressed one in the neighborhood. My family, and Barbie, adored their homemade clothes sewn with love.

I poured my heart into sewing with perfection. I chose my colors and fabrics and altered patterns to fit my desired style. I made bedspreads and drapes, and mended anything that needed fixing. Never bored, I always found something to do.

In addition to my clothes, my family loved my meals, including my special white bean soup. Since the American way of cooking emphasized quick and easy, I bought a blender to puree my cooked vegetables into tasty soups. I never cooked turnips. I'd had plenty when I was a refugee.

My social network grew as I established close friends in the community. Since I had traveled to many countries, I learned that underneath, we were all alike. It didn't matter whether a person was Jewish, Catholic, Protestant, French, Spanish, or Cuban. I had been treated kindly by many people from different cultures and religions. In return, I tried to practice the same kindness.

During this time, I didn't get to see much of my sisters. They and my mother carried on the tradition of moving. While living in Brazil, Willy married an American, and Mary married a man from Switzerland. They all eventually moved to America where they raised their families. My mother spent time with my family off and on, but would return to Brazil where she had many friends.

The only person from the army whom I saw after the war was my dear friend, Boudina. At one point, George and I took our children to meet her and the family in Santa Barbara, California. At our fond reunion, Boudina and I shared stories and laughed about the funny moments in the army, like the time we arrived late at the camp after a night out with our dates and jumped into our beds, still wearing our clothes and shoes, to avoid getting caught during inspection. Boudina was the first person with whom I had shared my secrets. I would have wanted to reveal more secrets to her, but as it often happened, family life took over. Sadly, we never met again.

The past still haunted me like a ghost. My children may have felt it, and there were times I forgot about it, but it always remained in the background. Sometimes, an event would trigger a memory of the war. My son, Paul, reminded me of an incident that occurred when he was twenty years old, working at a department store. A customer had been apprehended for writing bad checks, and Paul was scheduled for a court appearance. A sheriff arrived at the house to deliver a subpoena, giving notice that Paul had to testify in the case. When George saw the officer walking toward the house, he grabbed my arm and cried, "What are we going to do? What are we going to do?" Apparently, he flashed back to a time when Jews were hauled from their homes.

I tried to suppress the haunting memories in order to make the home safe for the children. They grew up knowing they were loved and cared for and able to take advantage of the many opportunities to establish careers. Paul became a psychologist, and Vivian received a master's degree in orientation mobility, to work with the blind. George and I were so happy about raising two wonderful children. Their many achievements made us proud.

I never anticipated that I would need all these blessings to help me deal with my greatest loss.

*Practice kindness to people, no matter
their culture or religion.*

Buena Park, California, 1979.

Last family photo with George, Yvonne, Vivian, and Paul.

Chapter Fifteen

MORE LOSSES

Losing a loving partner is like losing part of yourself.

George and I had just downsized and moved into our new home in Buena Park. With our children grown up and living successfully on their own, we planned to enjoy life and grow old together. Then again, the war taught me that life was unpredictable and that precious possessions, family life, and loved ones could be lost in an instant.

In 1978, I faced terrible losses. Willy died at the age of fifty-six after battling cancer for eight years. The sister who comforted me when I was a small child was gone from my life.

Then I received an even greater blow: my first and only real love was diagnosed with leukemia.

I hated that fateful day when George underwent tests at Studebaker Hospital because he wasn't feeling well. He rarely complained about ailments, so I knew it must've been serious. When he told me that the results revealed something about a high count of white blood cells, I guessed the diagnosis. Before the doctor could say anything, I asked if it was leukemia. The doctor confirmed my worst nightmare.

George and I had escaped the Nazis, survived as refugees, battled hunger and illness, and multiple deportations. I hadn't expected to face a life-threatening illness with my fifty-one-year-old husband. Both of us left the hospital in shock.

When we arrived home, we said very little. Neither of us knew how long he would live. The only thought that went through my mind was that I had to enjoy the rest of my time with my loving partner. I immediately suggested that we travel together while he still had the strength. George's reply was typical. He shook his head and told me that he didn't want to touch our money because he wanted me to be well looked after when he died.

I persisted. "You're more important than money. I want to travel and be with you."

George eventually agreed. He would cut back on his insurance business and see the world with me. But first, he had to share the difficult news with our children. Like me, they were shocked to hear about the leukemia. They came back home to spend time with their father. George and I felt comforted by Paul and Vivian. They organized a professional photographer to take a family picture, our last together. The two tall men, George and my son, stood behind me and my daughter. Both men rested a hand on our shoulders, with George's on mine and Paul's on his younger sister. We proudly displayed that photo on our wall.

While George suffered with the disease over three and a half years, we managed a number of special trips. I wanted him to see Australia and Indonesia, where I served in the army, so we packed his countless bottles of pills and started our travels. We began with a five-week tour that started in Hawaii and then went on to Australia, China, Thailand, Indonesia, and Japan. The wonderful collection of people on the tour helped create an incredible experience. Everyone seemed to get along as we visited fascinating places.

George's favorite was Sydney, Australia. Our hotel room overlooked the harbor and the renowned Opera House. Though we didn't get a chance to take in a performance, we toured the inside of the Opera House and later enjoyed a stroll around the beautiful harbor. George didn't feel any pain, but had a check-up in Sydney to make sure he could endure the rest of the vacation. The doctor gave him the okay to continue and refused payment for the visit. Like so many people on that trip, the doctor treated George and me with generosity and kindness.

When we traveled to Melbourne, we visited a country farm where we ate a beautiful steak dinner and watched a boxing match between the farmer and a trained kangaroo. Both wore boxing gloves and delighted the crowd with a punching match. The other kangaroos on the land were far from shy as they greedily searched men's pockets and women's purses, looking for goodies. It was another marvelous experience.

In China, we wandered around Tiananmen Square in Beijing and walked the Great Wall. I lost my grip on the wall and almost fell off. Fortunately, a man from the tour caught me before I tumbled over. Someone in the group was always lending a helping hand.

During our five weeks on the road, I loved watching George smile and laugh. It brought me tremendous joy.

We took other trips overseas, but the last one brought us to Central America because George wanted to see the Mayan pyramids. Strangely, I was the one who became ill on that vacation, picking up an intestinal bug. That ended our travels outside the United States.

As the disease progressed, we spent our traveling days going to and from the hospital. I hated to see George lose weight and spend his time sleeping.

In 1981, I found him barely moving in our upstairs bedroom. Mustering whatever strength I could manage, I pulled him onto my back and carried him downstairs. I then placed him in the car and drove him to St. Jude's Hospital where the staff took good care of him. George and I ended up celebrating our wedding anniversary in his hospital room. The oncologist, Dr. Justus, ordered two small cakes to commemorate the thirty-three years we had spent together as man and wife.

Paul, Vivian, and I spent the remaining days with George in the hospital. He released his final breath at the age of fifty-five. When he died, I was at the point of collapsing, knowing I would no longer dance or travel again with my husband.

He had been my trusted friend and partner, a man whom I loved and cared for deeply. We had laughed, danced, bickered, traveled, loved, and created a family from the ruins of war. Though we had agreed never to talk about the past horrors of escaping and surviving as refugees, I felt comforted, knowing that he shared similar experiences. I didn't feel alone with my secrets as long as I had George.

After he died, I carried those burdens on my own. The loving memories of George and my children gave me strength, but nonetheless, I had to face my most difficult loss alone.

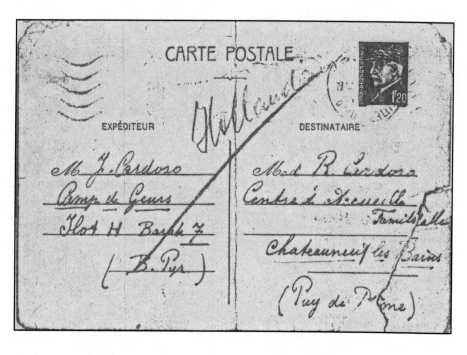

Jozef Cardozo's postcard addressed to his wife, Rachel.

Chapter Sixteen

SECRET POSTCARDS

Sometimes, it's very hard to look at the past.

A Jewish service took place shortly after George's death. I looked to my children for support during this painful time. According to his wishes, George's ashes were scattered on land and at sea, a fitting tribute to a man who had lived in many countries, like me.

I wondered if I could survive without my partner. I had done so in the past during the horrific times of war, but this was far different. Living with George for thirty-three years created security and comfort. He provided for me and the family, and I relied on him to be there. It felt as if I had lost part of myself.

I had lived in fear the past three years and four months. Fear of George dying, of grieving another death, of being alone. After spending many hours in the hospital, worrying about losing my husband, I needed quiet time to be at peace and sift through the many memories. I couldn't sleep at night, so I spent the early morning alone with the memories. I reminisced about George and my family with the children. I even thought about the war, the escape, and survival. But most of all, I dwelt on the love lost with George gone from my life.

My children were very supportive and wanted to help, but I encouraged them to get on with their lives. I didn't want them to suffer. I had experienced plenty of suffering and knew that death would eventually touch us all. I lost countless relatives to the concentration camps and faced the loss of my brother, father, sister, and now my husband. I wanted the grief to go away. It felt as if I was back in Europe during the war. Just like then, I had to push myself forward to survive.

During the first two months, I didn't want to leave the house or visit anyone, though I was invited out on many occasions. My children, good friends, and neighbors checked to see how I was doing. That definitely helped. Since my way of coping with grief was to get busy, I began to sort through George's belongings.

I started going through his business papers. Having been an insurance agent for many years, he kept plenty of documents. Plus, he was a saver. Before he died, George told me that he felt guilty about leaving me with all the insurance papers. I spent many long hours sifting through those documents, deciding what to keep and what to let go.

Once I organized the business matters, I delved into the private papers. Six months after George passed away, I found the postcards and letters from his father, Jozef Cardozo, who wrote to his wife, Rachel, and son when he was taken to the deportation camps before dying in a concentration camp. George was sixteen when his forty-one-year-old father wrote his final words.

Antwerp, Belgium, 1924.

Wedding of Jozef and Rachel Cardozo.

George had received the letters after his mother passed away and translated them from Dutch into English. They were extremely painful to read, for they revealed the love of a father toward his wife and only child, not knowing he was being deported to the death camp. I didn't realize it then that these heart-wrenching postcards would provide valuable clues about the final days of my brother.

The letters recorded Jozef's love, courage, and concern for his family. His first postcard, dated February 26, 1943, told of his trip to Gurs, a French internment camp in the Southwest of France. At that time, George was serving in the Maquis, the French resistance, and his mother was living in a Dutch refugee house in Southern France. His father and the men from the house had been taken by the French police and were told that they would be deported to a work camp.

In her book, *Wherever They May Be,* Beate Klarsfeld talked about that roundup and deportation of foreign male Jews from the unoccupied zone of France during February/March 1943, when Jozef was taken. According to Klarsfeld, there was a reprisal for the murder on February 13, 1943 of two German air force officers. Two thousand male Jews between the ages of sixteen and sixty-five were arrested. Those Jews were deported first to Gurs, then on to Drancy, and ultimately to Auschwitz.[1]

Using their nicknames, Jozef addressed his wife as Chel and his son as Jos. He himself signed his letters as JO. He managed to send a number of postcards to mark his journey. In his first letter, he wrote:

Dear Chel and Jos, I write this card in the train a little at a time every time it comes to a stop, and it happens quite often. It is a local train. We slept well last night on a clean straw mattress with blankets. We are going to Gurs. From there, we apparently are going to go to work.

Do not be surprised if you do not hear from me regularly. You know how the postal communications are. They think that we will arrive only by Saturday. This morning we received bread, sausage, and cheese for the trip. Sufficient. I hope that you have as much hope as I have. It cannot last much longer. In case that there are some wives who do not have any news from their husbands, we are all together, and we hope that we will remain that way.

We are in a good compartment with leather cushions. Our escorts are very friendly, which turned out better than we expected, and we were scared that they would not be. We departed at 7:00 a.m. this morning and ate at 8:00 a.m. The butter you gave me is delicious, and I use it sparingly, because I don't think I will get it soon.

I cannot give you my address because I do not know anything for sure. As soon as I know something I will write you at once. Maybe you can send me a pair of pants. Above all do not send me any money until I ask for it. I hope to write you again tomorrow. Tell Mrs. Boekbinder that her husband is with me, in case his postcard did not reach its destination. Also the ladies Goudeketting. Many kisses for you and Jos. Best regards to the families. JO

The next postcard, dated February 27, 1943, recorded his train trip:

Dear Chel and Jos, I write this card while still in the train because I do not know if I can write in Gurs when I arrive. You understand that as soon as I can, I will write. We are less than an hour from the camp. Our spirits are good and we hope for the best.... Our escorts who don't know much tell us that we are going to be put to work somewhere. That should not be too bad. It is not that easy to sleep in the train, but it is bearable. Early this morning we had coffee, just outside the station.

I hope that you can adapt yourselves to this new situation. On my part I do my best to do so. Pretty soon everything is going to be over and then we will be together again. We stood it this long. A little more is of no importance. Dear Chel and Jos keep courage and hold your heads high. Everything will be all right in the end. Give my regards to App and Duys and their wives. Do not write me as long as you do not know my address, because it would get lost anyway. I kiss you both in thought and will stop writing. JO

Chel, be careful when you write because of censorship, etc.

Jozef, like the others, were given false hope by being constantly told they were going to work someplace. At Auschwitz, the Germans placed a sign, a cruel joke, welcoming those who arrived by train, "*Arbeit Macht Frei:* Work makes (you) free."

Jozef continued to send word to his wife and son. In his next card, dated, February 28, 1943, Jozef told Rachel and his son that he arrived in Gurs, an internment camp for prisoners to be sent by train to the camp at Drancy on the outskirts of Paris. He mentioned that the Dutch and Belgians were no longer exempt from being deported.

Dear Chel and Jos, We arrived here Saturday afternoon and it was nearly dark when we got to our places in the barrack. We're the only Dutch in the whole camp and upon further inquiry it seems that the exception to the measures for the Dutch and Belgians do not hold anymore. Before long we will be put to work, but we do not know where.

We are working with a Protestant lady. She will try something for us because Protestants do not have to leave. We shall see, although we hold out little hope. Parcels that you might send me take long and therefore I do not know if I shall receive them here. Bread and hard-boiled eggs do not spoil. If I should be gone by then, these parcels would be returned to you. I don't have much to write to you. They do not fatten you here, but I have not gone hungry yet....

If I can, I will send you my ring and my watch chain.... Many kisses for you and Jos. Till later. Keep good hope. I keep my head high. JO

His next postcard was written the same day:

My very dears, We arrived here yesterday. I slept well. They say that we will not stay here very long. We will go to work somewhere, but we do not know where. Do not worry. It will probably be some time before you will hear from me. Do not lose courage. I am very optimistic. You will see that everything will work out.... I leave you for now and kiss you 1000 times. Your husband JO

Jozef mentioned in a postcard dated March 2, 1943 that he was sending a package. Prisoners were sometimes permitted to write to their families to create the illusion they were being relocated to a work camp. He must've suspected that he might not return. I included an excerpt:

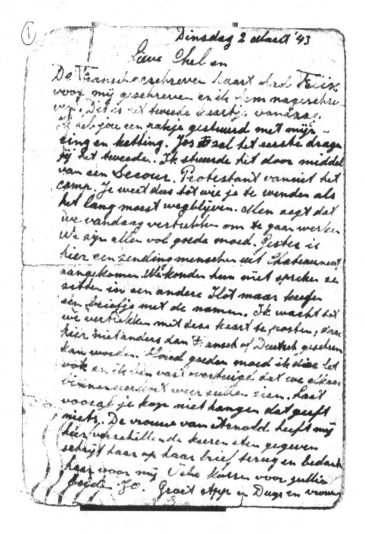

Jozef's postcard written in Dutch on March 2, 1943.

I send you a package today with my ring and watch chain. Jos is to wear the first and you the second. I sent it by means of a Protestant Aid Organization in the camp. You know where to go if it should take too long to arrive. They say that we leave today to go working. We are all full of good heart….

In his March 5, 1943 card, Jozef indicated that he was deported to another transit camp at Drancy. His card was brief:

Chel and Jos, I am at Drancy since yesterday and I will leave tomorrow for another camp, destination unknown. I'm in good health and my morale is very good. I hope you also will have confidence. I wish with all my heart to see you soon and at its best. Stay strong while waiting for the happiness to be together again. I embrace both of you very much. JO

Note the stamp on the left hand corner, showing mail was censured by the prefect of police and the censorship bureau.

Drancy Camp was under the control of the French police until July 3, 1943 when the Germans took over. The multi-story complex was built to hold 700 people, yet often held more than 7,000 inmates. I hate to imagine what Jozef and my brother went through.

After spending a few days in Drancy, Jozef was sent on train Convoy 51 on March 6, 1943 along with my brother and cousin, Raymond. According to Klarsfeld, 1002 male Jews aged sixteen to sixty-five comprised that convoy.[2]

They were probably treated the same way as other Jews who were locked in cattle cars meant to hold fifty people. Seventy to eighty people, sometimes more, were squashed into a compartment. Most of them carried a suitcase, for they were told they were being resettled. The average train trip to the concentration camp took three days. Without food, water, or toilets, many died from the heat during the summer, while others froze to death in the winter. Animals wouldn't be treated that way.

In his final postcard, March 7, 1943, Jozef tried to be hopeful but, clearly, he sensed the end. He wrote:

Dear Chel and Jos, We are on a journey but we do not know where. We are full of good courage. I hope that you too keep up your morale. Above all, do not let go of your courage. We are not either. We are all together in one carriage. The brothers V. Dantzig send their regards to everyone. Also the Goudeketting. Those who can escape, in my opinion, are best off. Many kisses from me. JO

At the end of the postcard, Jozef said, "Those who can escape, in my opinion, are best off." According to Klarsfeld, "The Auschwitz archives record the fate of Convoys 50 and 51. As soon as they arrived on March 6 and 8, all the men in them were gassed."[3]

At the death camps, those marked for extermination were told to strip and leave their belongings so they could enter the shower room. Instead of water, the Nazis poured in Zyklon B, a cyanide-based pesticide used to kill Jews more quickly.

Reading the postcards hit me hard. I understood how painful it was for George to talk about the war. He was very close to his father. Translating those letters from Dutch to English would have been unbearable for him. Every time I reviewed them, I felt extreme pain and wondered about my brother.

I realized that these cards were important historical documents. To commemorate George's father and family, I donated the original postcards to the Simon Wiesenthal Center in Los Angeles. (See acknowledging letter in Appendix B.)

*Death will eventually touch us all, so get
the most out of each day.*

*Yvonne's last needlepoint project, The Night Watch,
a replica of a painting by Rembrandt.*

Chapter Seventeen

LIFE AFTER GEORGE

If you feel you can't go any further, try harder.

Letting go of the past and moving forward continued to be difficult. One year after George died, I made a decision about the wedding rings. We had purchased the simple gold bands for our 1948 wedding in Antwerp, each buying a ring for the other. I wanted to melt both of them into a gold nugget to signify that after all the years we spent together, we were joined as one. I fastened the nugget on one of George's gold chains and lovingly placed it around my neck. That nugget will remain there as long as I live.

Still holding onto the memories of my husband, I eventually, reluctantly, went out with friends. Being with those who were married reminded me that George was gone. I wasn't sure how long it took, though it felt like forever, but I started to pick up the pieces and move forward. I started playing bridge again, something George and I relished. I thought about him often as we passed the cards. George was an excellent bridge player. Together we made a formidable team—just like in life. Without my partner, I had to keep on going.

I volunteered as a lay counselor at the Exchange Club Child Abuse Prevention Center where I worked with families with abused children. I wanted to feel productive again and make a contribution. Helping needy children, though difficult, proved to be very rewarding. Holding the hand of a little girl hungry for affection warmed my heart.

Another activity that helped me deal with my grief was dancing, something George and I also enjoyed. I took lessons at an Arthur Murray dance studio and learned new steps for the freestyle, the tango, and the Viennese Waltz. Dancing provided me with a form of therapy to occupy my mind.

One and a half years after George passed away, I traveled overseas. I visited Belgium and met old friends from the Maccabi Club. I had planned on visiting Ghent, but the memories of the frantic escape when I was twelve years old haunted me. The city was the place where I saw the bombs fall on the train and heard that the Nazis were on their way. When I made my way to Ghent, it began to rain. The dreary wet sky stopped me in my tracks. I couldn't go back there. I had experienced enough loss in my life and couldn't bear more painful memories. I turned around and returned to Antwerp, my place of birth.

When I returned to California, I found a job as a cashier at Nordstrom, then sold kitchenware in a department store near my home. I also returned to needlework and finished my last needlepoint project, *The Night Watch,* a replica of one of the best known paintings by the Dutch painter, Rembrandt. I kept myself busy and took the occasional vacation overseas.

No matter what I did, I still thought of George. Many years after he passed away, I had a dream that he flew down from the skylight. I felt his presence in the bedroom and became scared when he sat on the bed. It moved, causing my heart to beat wildly. I told him, "You shouldn't be here."

He replied, "I know, but I want to see how you're doing."

"I'm doing fine," I quickly answered.

Then he flew away through the skylight. As I saw him leave, I yelled, "I want to talk. Come back. Come back."

But he was gone.

That dream startled me so much I leapt of bed and stared at the skylight. I couldn't go back to sleep. I felt sad that he left me again. My heart remained heavy.

Fortunately, there were memorable celebrations to lift my spirits. I proudly attended my children's weddings. I flew to Georgia for Paul's marriage to Patty, and several years later, attended Vivian's wedding to David in Monterey, California. The two happy occasions brought joy to my life.

I remained in California where I have lived in the same comfortable home for the past twenty-two years. After my mother's second husband died, she moved into a retirement community nearby. I assumed the responsibility for her care and often visited her, sometimes five to six times a week. I rarely felt appreciated for all that I did, but that was my mother. She lived a difficult life. She spent her remaining years in convalescence and died at the age of ninety-two. My other sister, Mary, died nine years later, leaving me as the last member of my immediate family.

While I still think of George and all the wonderful times we had together and with our children, I am grateful for having a full life. I still cook soup and play bridge, but no longer work with my hands. A number of my friends who heard about my ordeals kept telling me over the years, "Write the book."

After putting it off for quite some time, I decided to find out what happened to my brother. I asked my son to search the Internet for any information about Marcel. Miraculously, pieces of the puzzle came in documents that helped form a picture of my brother's final days. His name was included on the register of victims on train Convoy 51 that left Drancy, the internment camp. I was shocked to see Marcel's name on the same list that included George's father. (See Appendix C.)

Strangely, Jozef's postcards provided a glimpse into my brother's final days. The records indicated that Marcel went straight to Gurs, then onto Drancy, both deportation camps in France, where some 70,000 prisoners were processed during the war. On March 6, 1943, two days after his twentieth birthday, he was scheduled to ride the same death train, Convoy 51, as George's father, Jozef Cardozo, and my cousin, Raymond van Loon. However, Marcel escaped but was recaptured. To this day, I don't know what happened to my brother, but can only assume that once he was captured, he was shot or died in a death camp. I still have occasional nightmares of Nazis beating Marcel after he was caught.

Perpignan, France, 1942.

The last picture taken of Marcel at nineteen.

I often wonder what George would have thought if he knew his father had traveled the same route as my brother. I regret not talking with my husband about all that we had endured, but now recognize the importance of telling my story. It was time to record the difficult events that shaped my life.

It is never too late to break the silence and share secrets. If we learn the lessons from the past, future generations can live in a world where there is peace.

If you feel overwhelmed by problems, consider helping others who are in greater need.

Hope lives when people remember.

- Simon Wiesenthal

Epilogue

NEVERMORE

A new generation can live in a world of peace when we say to war, "Nevermore."

As I reflect on my life and the many places I have lived — Belgium, the Netherlands, France, Spain, Jamaica, West Indies, Cuba, Australia, Indonesia, Canada, and America — I have come to appreciate the diversity of people who have different colors and nationalities. No matter where I went, I encountered acts of kindness from those who were brought up in a different religion or culture.

We are all the same underneath. So I have a difficult time understanding how a country like Germany could exterminate a race of people because of religion. Nine and a half million Jews had resided in Europe before the Holocaust. Two-thirds were killed. Three million men, two million women, and one million children died in the Holocaust, just because they were Jewish.[4]

About 140,000 Jews lived in the Netherlands at the beginning of the war. Persecution of Dutch Jews started shortly after the occupation, with mass deportations occurring in 1942. Of the 100,000 Jewish deportees, many of whom were sent to concentration camps, most were killed. Less than twenty-five percent of Dutch Jews survived.[5]

One who did not survive was Anne Frank. She wrote her famous diary while hiding from the Germans after they occupied the Netherlands. At the age of thirteen, she was forced to hide with her family in Amsterdam to avoid being caught by the Nazis. In her diary, she broke the silence and revealed her thoughts and secrets. She spent two years concealed in a secret annex of a building located at 263 Prinsengracht. When she was captured in August 1944, she was transported to a prison and later to a concentration camp. Though she died in 1945, her inspiring words live on today.

I was twelve when the Germans invaded the Netherlands and Belgium and consider myself fortunate to have escaped the

Nazis and the death camps. Many members of my family did not survive. The trauma of living in fear and the pain of losing family members was so overwhelming that it seemed easier to be silent and keep the secrets buried.

No one should have to hide or bury secrets. The price was heavy and the burden great. I felt compelled to reveal my secrets, the pain of living with past memories that were not shared. I still remember that six aunts and six uncles, plus their spouses and all their children, less two, died in Auschwitz or Sobibór. Almost fifty relatives perished in concentration camps.

George passed away before information became available that showed where and how his father died. He never knew about the strange coincidence of my brother riding the same train. My husband may have been comforted with some closure, knowing the place and time of death. I would definitely feel more at peace if I knew how and where my brother died.

At the end of World War II, there were estimates of some three million Holocaust survivors. These were Jews who had either lived in a country under the Nazi regime, who had fled a country due to the Nazi occupation, or who were refugees or in hiding during the war. One document showed that one million survivors were alive in 2003.[6] It is difficult to know how many exist today.

Each survivor has a significant story; mine is just one of them. Our personal details provide ongoing proof to those who would ever question the Holocaust or whether Jews, gypsies, the disabled, or homosexuals were exterminated. If only the doubters could experience the horrors of the Nazi terror, forced labor camps, mass deportations, and cruel deaths of loved ones, they would never question the reality of Hitler's final solution.

The war took a lot out of me. While it has been painful and difficult to break my silence, dredge up horrible memories, and share my secrets, the truth had to be told before I could rest in peace. No one should experience such horrors. No one should live in fear or be killed because of their religion, nationality, or color.

I can only hope that my story acts as a reminder for the world to say, "This will happen nevermore!"

Appendix A

NETHERLANDS FORCES INTELLIGENCE SERVICE
(NEFIS)

NEW ZEALAND INSURANCE BUILDING
334-338 QUEEN STREET, BRISBANE

NO. REB/101

ENCLOSURES:

TEL. U 7076
U 7077
U 7078

SUBJECT: Letter of Commendation.

DATE: 26.3.1946.

TO WHOM IT MAY CONCERN.

1. Corporal YVONNE DE LEEUWE, V.K.166 (Netherlands Womens' Army)
    has worked in Netherlands Forces Intelligence Service (NEFIS)
    from 1st September 1945 until 27 March 1946.

2. During this period I have known her personally. She has
    served in the NEFIS cypher-room as a clerk cyphering and decypher-
    ing messages that were sent or received in code, had to enter
    telegrams, pass them thru, and type them out on the official
    telegram forms. She handled the teletype-machine several
    times with good success, but is still lacking the experience
    that is necessary for a qualified teletype operator. I have
    found her to be conscientious, always willing to carry out
    instructions to the best of her ability.

3. I have had an opportunity as Officer in charge of NEFIS Code
    Room to observe this Corporal carefully in the performance of
    her duties and would recommend her to anybody desirous of the
    services of a girl for the same kind of duty or general office
    work.

W.M. van der VEUR,
Lt.Comdr.,
R.Neth.Navy Res.,
Representative Director NEFIS
    in Australia.

Letter of Commendation from NEFIS

Appendix B

SIMON WIESENTHAL CENTER
on the campus of yeshiva university of los angeles

June 7, 1982

Ms. Yvonne Carson
10 Candlewood Way
Buena Park, CA   90621

Dear Mrs. Carson:

On behalf of the Simon Wiesenthal Center,
I wish to thank you for the post cards (and
translations) which you generously donated.
You can be assured that we will set aside an
appropriate space in our museum for their viewing.

Thank you again for your support of the
Center in our efforts to keep the memory of the
Holocaust alive.

Cordially,

Alex Grobman

Alex Grobman, Ph.D.
Director

/rj

P. S.   Per your request, we enclose herewith
2 copies of each of the documents.

9760 west pico boulevard, los angeles, california 90035   (213) 553-9036

Letter of Recognition from Simon Wiesenthal Center

142

Appendix C

CARDOZO	HAIM	23.05.02	AMSTERDAM	HOL	✡
CECHMAN	JACOB	.07	VARSOVIE	P	
CECHMAN	JOSEPH	11.02.04	VARSOVIE	IND	
CERF	SIMON	21.02.05	HABAYLA WEND	B	
CHABIELSKI	POSZEK	05.11.05	LASKA	P	
CHAIMOWITZ	JOSEPH	26.02.89	WAVITARNES	P	
CHAIMA	JANKIEL	18.06.04	JELLES	P	
CHALPERN	MOSZEK	05.05.98	LODZ	P	
CHAPIRO	MARC	21.05.03	LITINE	R	
CHAPNIKOFF	JACOB	01.02.94	KAINITZA	R	
CHARASCH	ABRAHAM	16.06.89	ROUNO	R	
CHARYTON	SZMYL	13.05.06	SIENNOV	P	
CHASZWALV	STRUL	15.05.01	KAZIMISEH	R	
CHERSIN	SIMON	12.09.82	BOTOSANI	RO	
CHEZINSKI	HILLER	15.02.05	KOUSKY	P	
CHLEWICKI	HENRI	22.03.21	OFFENBACH	APA	
CHUR	JOYE	31.12.94	VARSOVIE	P	
CHURINSKI	KURT	30.12.17	BERLIN	A	
CISINSKI	SZMEREK	24.04.15	KALUSZIN	P	
COHEN	ALBERT	10.10.23	SALONIQUE	G	
COHEN	BARUCH	12.03.95	THESSALONIKI	G	
COHEN	MATHIEV	21.03.98	VARSOVIE	R	
COVENCA	DARIO	20.08.03	SALONIQUE	G	
COVO	SAM	01.05.99	SALONIQUE	G	
CUKIER	CHIL	24.06.99	KOZENICE	P	
CUKIER	SIOMA	13.07.11	KOVEL	P	
CUKIERMAN	JACQUES	13.05.24	KALUSZIN	P	
CYTRYNOWICZ	CEDAL	06.02.00	OPOTENO	P	
CYTRYNOWICZ	MAURICE	25.10.23	ALTONA	P	
CYWIE	PINKUS	20.08.93	GABERI	P	
CZCZERBATY	SOJNA	04.04.97	KOWEL	P	
DANCYGIER		01.09.00	SCZIKOCINY	IND	
DAREVSKY	SALOMON	18.05.00	ODESSA	R	
DAUMAN	BENOIST	18.09.24	ANVERS	B	
DAUMAN	JOSEPH	18.09.22	ANVERS	B	
DAVID	HERSCH	16.07.88	JASSY	RO	
DAVIDOV	OSIP	26.01.98	ODESSA	R	
DAVIDOVITCH	SZCHLAMA	04.07.04	POLOGNE	P	
DAVIDS	ANDRIES	12.10.16	ROTTERDAM	HOL	
DAVIDSOHN	FRITZ	12.10.06	HAMBOURG	A	
DAVIDSON	GITIEL	25.01.99	ODESSA	R	
DAVIDSON	MORDOKO	25.01.99	ODESSA	R	
DAVIDOWICZ	HEINZ	10.07.24	DUSSELDORF	P	
DAWIDOWICZ	OJLE	11.08.06	SOSNOWICE	P	
DE LEEUWE	SAL	04.03.23	AMSTERDAM	HOL	✡

Excerpt from a French deportation document that listed the names and birth dates of those on Convoy 51. See Haim (Jozef) Cardozo listed at the top of the page with Sal (Marcel) de Leeuwe at the bottom.[7]

Appendix D

De Leeuwe Family Tree

Yvonne de Leeuwe's Paternal Grandparents

Abraham de Leeuwe	**Married**	**Mina Hamburg**
1867-1942	1888-1934	1872-1934
Died: Auschwitz, Poland		Died: Amsterdam

Seven Children:

1. Levie   1888- ?   Date and place of death unknown
2. Esther   1890-1942   Died: Auschwitz, Poland
3. Roosje   1891-1942   Died: Auschwitz, Poland
4. Henriette   1893-1943   Died: Sobibór, Poland
5. **Jacob**   **1895-1953**   **Died: Rio de Janeiro, Brazil**
6. Flora   1898-1943   Died: Sobibór, Poland
7. Maurits   1900-1969   Died: Sluis, Netherlands

Yvonne de Leeuwe's Maternal Grandparents

Salomon van Loon	**Married**	**Marianne Bonewit**
1863-1911	1887-1911	1864-1940

Ten Children:

1. Joseph   1888-1956   Died: Antwerp, Belgium
2. Clara   1889-1942   Died: Auschwitz, Poland
3. Isaac   1892-1943   Died: Auschwitz, Poland
4. Vogeltje   1894-1896   Died: Amsterdam, Netherlands
5. Hijman   1895-1943   Died: Sobibór, Poland
6. Philip   1897-1943   Died: Seibersdorf, Austria
7. Vogelina   1899-1943   Died: Auschwitz, Poland
8. **Elisabeth**   **1902-1995**   **Died: California, USA**
9. Nathan   1904-1943   Died: Auschwitz, Poland
10. Louis   1909-1944   Died: Auschwitz, Poland

Yvonne de Leeuwe's Parents:

Jacob de Leeuwe	Married	Elisabeth van Loon
1895-1953	1921-1953	1902-1995
Died: Rio de Janeiro, Brazil	Amsterdam	Died: California, USA

Four Children:

1. Wilhelmina 1921-1978   Died: California, USA
2. Sal   1923-1943   Died in a concentration camp
3. Mary   1924-2011   Died: Florida, USA
4. **Yvonne**   **1927-Present**

George Cardozo's Parents

Jozef Haim Cardozo	Married	Rachel Cohen De Lara
1902-1943	Belgium	1902-1973
Died: Auschwitz, Poland		Died: Montreal, Canada

Child:

1. **George**   **1926-1981**   **Died: California, USA**

George Cardozo and Yvonne de Leeuwe

George Cardozo	Married	Yvonne de Leeuwe
Changed name to Carson		
1948-1981	1948-1981	1927-Present
Died: California, USA	Antwerp	Lives – California, USA

Two Children:

1. Paul   1951-Present
2. Vivian   1955-Present

Notes

1. Klarsfeld, Beate, *Wherever They May Be,* New York: Vanguard Press, 1972, p. 107.

2. Klarsfeld, Beate, *Wherever They May Be,* New York: Vanguard Press, 1972, p. 109.

3. Klarsfeld, Beate, *Wherever They May Be,* New York: Vanguard Press, 1972, p. 109.

4. Halevy, Yechiam, *Historical Atlas of the Holocaust: Holocaust Memorial Museum,* New York: Macmillan Publishing, 1996, p. 221.

5. Halevy, Yechiam, *Historical Atlas of the Holocaust: Holocaust Memorial Museum,* New York: Macmillan Publishing, 1996, pp. 118-119.

6. Dellapergola, Prof. Sergio, "Review of Relevant World Demographic Information on World Jewry," Final Report Presented to the International Commission on Holocaust Era Insurance Claims, Jerusalem, 2003, p. 6.

7. Klarsfeld, Serge, *Memorial to the Jews deported from France, 1942-1944: documentation of the deportation of the victims of the Final Solution in France,* New York: B. Klarsfeld Foundation, 1983.

Acknowledgements

I want to recognize and offer my heartfelt thanks to the following people for helping me tell my story and publish this book.

My son, Paul, and daughter, Vivian, for their support and encouragement in writing this book. Paul conducted a lot of research about my brother and my father-in-law and helped find the missing pieces to what happened to Marcel. I'm also grateful for the support of Vivian's husband, David, and Paul's wife, Patty.

Leonard Szymczak, for the many hours he spent attempting to understand what my life was all about. His curiosity and unceasing research helped me better understand myself and the times in which I lived. He made it easier to relive my past. The process of writing this book brought back many memories, some of which were locked inside. With his grace and understanding, I learned how to unlock and appreciate them. Because of his help, I can now move forward with no more silence to bear and no more secrets to keep.

Rondi Brown, for her help in gathering historical information, organizing the maps, assisting with the photographer, and editing the manuscript.

Mary Harris, for reviewing, editing, and making suggestions to improve the book.

My nieces, Eleonor and Lilian, for their encouraging words of support.

Mari Frank, who contributed in her own special way.

And finally, to my friends who kept telling me, "Write your book!"

About the Author

Yvonne Carson-Cardozo was twelve years old when she and her family escaped the German occupation in Belgium. As a refugee, she traveled to France, Spain, Jamaica, and West Indies. After moving with her family to Cuba, she eventually joined the Dutch Indonesian Army. After three months of basic and overseas training in the United States, she served in Australia and Indonesia, working in the Netherlands Forces Intelligence Service, deciphering and encoding secret military telegrams.

Following the war, she lived in Belgium, Canada, and finally America, which she has called home for the past fifty-five years. Yvonne has two children and lives in California.

On Veteran's Day 2013, Yvonne received a Certificate of Recognition as the 2013 Veteran of the Year for the City of Mission Viejo. Yvonne was also recognized by the Senator of the 38th District of the Senate of California and the local congressman of the United States Congress.

For more information, visit Yvonne's website:

www.SilenceAndSecrets.com

Made in the USA
San Bernardino, CA
23 September 2018